In the Shadow
of the Shekinah

God's Journey With Us

ROY GANE

REVIEW AND HERALD® PUBLISHING ASSOCIATION

Since 1861 | www.reviewandherald.com

Unless otherwise indicated, Bible texts are from the New King James Version. Copyright © 1979, 1980, 1982 by Thomas Nelson, Inc. Used by permission. All rights reserved.

Scripture quotations marked NASB are from the *New American Standard Bible,* copyright © 1960, 1962, 1963, 1968, 1971, 1972, 1973, 1975, 1977, 1994 by The Lockman Foundation. Used by permission.

Texts credited to NIV are from the *Holy Bible, New International Version.* Copyright © 1973, 1978, 1984, International Bible Society. Used by permission of Zondervan Bible Publishers.

Bible texts credited to NRSV are from the New Revised Standard Version of the Bible, copyright © 1989 by the Division of Christian Education of the National Council of the Churches of Christ in the U.S.A. Used by permission.

Texts credited to Tanakh are from *Tanakh: A New Translation of the Holy Scriptures According to the Traditional Hebrew Text.* Copyright © The Jewish Publication Society of America, Philadelphia, 1985.

This book was
Edited by Gerald Wheeler
Copyedited by James Cavil
Cover designed by Ron J. Pride
Interior designed by Heather Rogers
Cover art by Lars Justinen, www.goodsalt.com
Typeset: Bembo11/14

PRINTED IN U.S.A.

13   12   11   10   09   5   4   3   2   1

Library of Congress Cataloging-in-Publication Data
Gane, Roy, 1955-   .
   In the shadow of the Shekinah: God's journey with us / Roy E. Gane.
      p. cm.
Bible. O.T. Numbers—Commentaries. I. Title.
BS1265.53.G36 2009
222'.14—dc22
                                        2009001245

ISBN 978-0-8280-2421-1

CONTENTS

INTRODUCTION

My teenage daughter and her friends are intensely interested in the character of God, especially as revealed in the Old Testament. When they sit around and frankly talk about how they personally relate to God, their questions often have to do with the way He acts. Why was He so hard on the Israelites and other peoples in ancient times? Was He fair to command the Israelites to exterminate whole nations, including women and innocent children? Can we trust and like such a God?

How thoughtful young people relate to such questions will have a major impact on their decisions to believe that there is a loving God and to allow Him to be part of their lives—or not. For them the options are not so much between one Christian denomination and another as between Christianity and agnosticism or practical atheism.

The present volume explores an Old Testament book that plays a central role in the discussion about God's character: Numbers. This book is strikingly relevant to our experience today as we journey toward unending life in the ultimate Promised Land: a new earth, the Paradise restored (Rev. 21; 22). But people have tended to neglect it, perhaps partly because its name has little appeal to anyone except accountants and mathematicians. "Numbers" refers to the census lists in chapters 1-4 and 26, which show how the entire first generation of Israelites who left Egypt, except for Caleb and Joshua, died in the wilderness because of their rebellion against God.

The Hebrew name of the book derives from its first verse: "In the Wilderness." This title refers to the setting during the decades that God led the Israelites from place to place in the desert regions between Mount Sinai and Canaan, the land that God had promised to them. Although it should have been the book that recounted the conquest of Canaan, it is instead about delay. The Israelites could have entered Canaan 40 years sooner than they did, but the adult generation failed to trust the Lord and show loyalty to Him, even after all the wonders that He had performed for them.

The Promised Land was God's gift to the Israelites. He had given them the title to ownership of it (Ex. 6:4; 32:13). They had to put forth the effort to cooperate with Him in order to possess it, but it was already theirs (Num. 13:30). However, their lack of faith and loyalty prevented them from receiving the gift. So the nation had to wait in the wilderness until the next generation was ready and the older generation died out.

Numbers is one of the most dramatic and tragic books in the Bible. The exhilarating expectation of a quick trip to the "land flowing with milk and honey" bogs down in complaints about food and then paralyzing fear of Canaanite giants with walled cities. A splendidly organized community implodes in revolt against the leadership of God through His servants, Moses and Aaron. Leaders of a mutiny and their families get swallowed alive by the earth, and Levites who try to usurp priestly function find themselves zapped by divine fire. Divine plagues against rebels become progressively more severe, with the body count reaching 24,000 when many were seduced into immorality and idolatrous worship of the Baal of Peor. Even Moses disobeys God by striking a rock instead of speaking to it to obtain water, so that the Lord has to forbid him to enter the Promised Land.

Amidst all the unnecessary strife, God's Shekinah ("Dwelling"/ "Resident") presence in the glory cloud hovering over the sanctuary watches over His faulty people and unfailingly provides them with the miracle of food from heaven (manna) every day. He organizes them for success, disciplines them, mercifully answers intercessory prayers for them when they rebel, provides ways for them to receive atonement and healing, protects them against curses, and gives them victory against enemies who would otherwise destroy them.

As the Israelites journeyed in the shadow of the Shekinah, how could anyone possibly question whether God was among them? Yet that is what the Israelites did again and again and again! Incredibly slow learners, they took many years just to get through the basic training of faith. Until they had that, God could not lead them across the Jordan River into Canaan, where their nation was to live according to His principles in order to reveal His character to all peoples of the earth. They had to be willing to serve as God's faithful witnesses if they were to receive His blessings. If He blessed them when they rebelled against Him, He would send the wrong message by reinforcing disloyalty.

The journey of Christians parallels that of the Israelites, as the apostle Paul recognized: "Moreover, brethren, I do not want you to be unaware that all our fathers were under the cloud, all passed through the sea, all were baptized into Moses in the cloud and in the sea, all ate the same spiritual food, and all drank the same spiritual drink. For they drank of that spiritual Rock that followed them, and that Rock was Christ. But with most of them God was not well pleased, for their bodies were scattered in the wilderness. Now these things became our examples, to the intent that we should not lust after evil things as they also lusted. And do not become idolaters as were some of them. . . . Nor let us tempt Christ, as some of them also tempted, and were destroyed by serpents; nor complain, as some of them also complained, and were destroyed by the destroyer. Now all these things happened to them as examples, and they were written for our admonition, upon whom the ends of the ages have come" (1 Cor. 10:1-11).

The book of Numbers teaches us how to live and journey with God, even under extreme circumstances. Good and worthy of our trust, He wants to lavish blessings upon us with His awesome power. He will never let us down if we wholeheartedly follow Him and acknowledge our total dependence on Him. But He holds us accountable for the way that we depict Him to others in the world, whom He wants to save. If we misrepresent Him, they will not find themselves drawn to Him. He is patient with the inhabitants of our planet and gives them a long time to repent (cf. Gen. 15:13-16), but He is committed to purifying our world from evil and oppression in order to make it safe for true, unselfish love (Rev. 19-22).

Like the ancient people of God, we have crises of faith, struggles about leadership, and deceptions that entice us to compromise our relationship with our Savior. Our goal is great and our hopes are high, but we too easily get distracted. Like the Israelites, we have delayed ourselves from entering our eternal home. Our progress has not always been forward. Looking up to God, we require a fresh vision of His big picture to keep us going. He provides for our daily needs and leads us step by step to a better land. But He does not force us to go, or to travel faster than we are willing. Instead, He encourages us that our promised home is an exceedingly good land, and by His strength we are well able to possess it (Num. 13:30; 14:7-9)!

The present volume is a fresh reading of Numbers for contemporary readers, one designed to illuminate key aspects of God's character and His way of leading faulty people. It is not a comprehensive commentary. For that I direct the reader to the author's *Leviticus, Numbers (NIV Application Commentary* [Grand Rapids: Zondervan, 2004]), which draws out many more details and life applications and provides extensive references to other works. For an introduction to the meaning of the Israelite sanctuary and its services, see also the author's *Altar Call* (Berrien Springs, Mich.: Diadem, 1999).

For the present book I have used the New King James Version (NKJV) as the primary English translation for scriptural quotations, referring to others by their abbreviations (NRSV, Tanakh, etc.). As a teacher of biblical languages, I derive my interpretations from study of the original Hebrew, Aramaic, and Greek texts that constitute the Bible. My choice of a translation does not indicate unqualified endorsement of any English version, because every translation in any language is a form of commentary produced through scholarly interpretation.

I am grateful to Rebecka Noble, my research assistant, for gathering many of the illustrations included in this book.

Chapter 1

One Nation Under God
(Numbers 1-4)

Organized Religion

After setting the Israelites free, God kept them in the Sinai wilderness for almost a year before leading them on toward Canaan (cf. Ex.19:1; Num. 10:11, 12). The area by Mount Sinai was away from military threats and the temptations of pagan societies. Here the Lord organized His people as a functioning nation with a dramatic system of worship so that they could cooperate with Him and each other in carrying out their mission (Ex. 29-Num. 10).

The Lord gave the Israelites a kind of "organized religion." Many people have rejected such religion:

• "This would be the best of all possible worlds if there were no religion in it."—John Adams, second president of the United States.

• "Religion is the opium of the people."—Karl Marx.

• "Religions? Endless arguments over trivial contradictions in books written by ignorant savages to explain thunder in the dark."—author unknown.

• "A society without religion is like a crazed psychopath without a loaded .45."—author unknown.

• "Organized religion is a sham and a crutch for weak-minded people who need strength in numbers. It tells people to go out and stick their noses in other people's business."—Jesse Ventura, governor of Minnesota, 1999.

• "Just in terms of allocation of time resources, religion is not

11

very efficient. There's a lot more I could be doing on a Sunday morning."—Bill Gates.

Unfortunately, those who make such statements can find ample support in thousands of years of religious history. To many, even if they wish to serve God, organization destroys true spirituality and pure devotion to Him. As evidence, they can cite numerous religious groups that are more focused on power and self-righteousness than on piety and service. Such people gain a greater blessing by themselves or with family members or close friends when they worship at home or out in God's nature than they do attending a stiff, shallow, or boring service or enduring the exclusion and criticism of toxic cliques.

I sympathize with the concerns of those who reject organized religion. My wife, Connie, and I studied for two years in Jerusalem, a center and birthplace of the three great monotheistic religions: Judaism, Christianity, and Islam. We have friends among all three groups and find many positive aspects in their beliefs and practices. But although we love Jerusalem, we witnessed a huge amount of religious antagonism, arrogance, and selfishness among the three faiths. Rather than love for others, religious traditions foster deep-seated prejudices that infect people from childhood. They seem to imbibe an adversarial sense of "us" versus "them" with their mother's milk.

Our most disturbing experience in Jerusalem was the "Ceremony of the Holy Fire" on Easter weekend in the Church of the Holy Sepulchre. Fifteen thousand "Christians" crowded into the ancient church housing the traditional site of Christ's crucifixion, burial, and resurrection.

The day was the Sabbath between Good Friday and Easter Sunday. A Christian "high priest" was to enter Christ's tomb, where the Holy Spirit was supposed to light his candle, and then he would share the "holy fire" with thousands of worshippers holding candles.

Connie and I and some friends went to the church early and found a place on a balcony overlooking the entrance. We were confined there for six hours. During the first couple hours while the outer doors of the church were open, we watched people entering. They belonged to two different "Christian" groups, each of whom resented the presence of the other. In fact, people told us that such animosity existed between the various Eastern Christian denominations sharing the Church of the Holy Sepulchre that the custodian of the key to the shrine is an Arab Muslim. The practice keeps the "Christians" from trying to take the key from one another by violence.

The Israeli police had placed a barrier down the center of the entrance to the church in order to separate the worshippers belonging to the two groups. Each faction had a line of strong young men stationed along the opposite walls of the entrance to guard their territorial rights. About every 15 minutes a scuffle broke out between those young men, and about every half hour a major brawl developed. Talk about "Christianity in action"!

A small, older woman entered on the wrong side. The imperious head priest who had jurisdiction over that side repeatedly turned her away, but for some reason she refused to go to the other side. Finally he grabbed her and shoved her hard. She sprawled full length on the stone pavement, screaming.

Look, I will be brutally frank. If all I knew of religion was what I had experienced in Jerusalem, the so-called holy city, I would probably be an atheist or agnostic. Much of organized "Christianity" has turned from the divine principle of love to the satanic principles of selfishness and hate. Other forms of religion have become baldly pagan and polytheistic or glorified occult.

But does all this mean that organization by itself necessarily destroys religion? Is disorganized or unorganized religion a better alternative? Should we be chaotic Christians? Or is it corruption of religious organization that is the problem?

In the Bible God's people enjoyed the fellowship and support of belonging to a group. The Israelites journeyed together. Jesus called a cluster of disciples, not detached hermits. They related to each other as well as to Him. Together we are stronger in our spiritual and practical lives than if we are isolated: "And let us consider one another in order to stir up love and good works, not forsaking the assembling of ourselves together, as is the manner of some, but exhorting one another, and so much the more as you see the Day approaching" (Heb. 10:24, 25).

13

Groups of people are happier and more effective if they do things in an orderly rather than disorganized way. When Christians come together for mutual encouragement, they profit more by speaking one at a time rather than all at once (1 Cor. 14:26-32). "For God is not the author of confusion but of peace" (verse 33). God values harmony and order, as shown by the order in His heavenly headquarters (Rev. 4; 5) and in His creation on Planet Earth (Gen. 1; 2).

To cooperate with God, the members of a group must be willing to work harmoniously with each other. Only when Christ's followers were unified could they receive the Holy Spirit's empowerment to take the gospel to the world (Acts 2).

Christ's commission to make disciples of all nations, baptizing and teaching them (Matt. 28:19, 20) is too big for any of us to do on our own. To fulfill it, we need each other with all the richness of our diversity, just as the parts of a human body require each other in order to accomplish their task of maintaining life. So the early Christian church organized its members according to the spiritual gifts or talents bestowed upon them by the Holy Spirit (1 Cor. 12; cf. Acts 6:1-7).

The greater the task and the larger the group carrying it out, the more we need effective organization. The Israelites comprised a large group, and their task of taking Canaan was monumental. Therefore, they needed an effective organization that would keep them pulling in the same direction. As a result the Lord directed Moses to conduct a military census that counted men of fighting age—at least 20 years old (Num. 1). The purpose was not simply to find out how many Israelites there were, but to organize an army.

The military census did not include the tribe of Levites (Num. 1:47-54). The leadership numbered them in a separate census that counted men who were 30 to 50 years of age—the prime of mature life—to serve the various needs of the sanctuary (Num. 4). The Lord's instructions regarding the duties of the Levites, and which Levites would perform them, were detailed. It was organized religion on a massive scale, and God Himself set it up.

Organization is not inherently bad. It is a neutral instrument that one can use for a good or bad purpose. People can assemble to assist victims of a hurricane, tsunami, or drought. Or they can exploit other people. The leaders and goals of an organization, including a religious one, determine its character.

The Right Kind of Organization

The nature of an organization should fit its purpose. A soccer club can be relatively uncomplicated, with flexible boundaries of membership, a relaxed security system, and a few rules to make sure that everyone gets treated fairly. An army or nation is a different matter. It must serve the complex interests of many people and deal with real danger from enemies, who are mostly outside, though some could be internal.

Modern readers of the book of Numbers tend to find the discipline imposed on the Israelites in their wilderness journey to be severe. But the entire nation became an army on the move. They needed military discipline to accomplish their objectives as safely as possible. Anyone who failed to cooperate could jeopardize the security of the entire group.

Sound familiar? People who travel by air these days must observe strict rules for the safety of everyone. Don't leave your baggage unattended. Don't accept packages from strangers. Limit the liquids and gels in your carry-on luggage. Such precautions are practical, not legalistic.

The Lord's system of organization was even more than that needed for a national army—it was nothing less than the DNA of a new world order. The purpose of the success and prosperity of God's chosen people, who were governed by wise and just laws in harmony with His loving character, was to attract other peoples (Deut. 4:5-8; cf. 1 Kings 10:1-13).

The divinely ordained system of organization, designed to support progress toward radical results, worked with existing social structures as much as possible. While the Lord wanted to transform people into harmony with His character, He did not engage in social engineering or revolution. Similarly, when we take the gospel to people of other cultures, we can work with their societies and ways of doing things to the extent that they do not conflict with divine principles. To evangelize does not mean to westernize or colonize. The apostle Paul recognized the value of such adaptability: "I have become all things to all men, that I might by all means save some" (1 Cor. 9:22).

Israelite society was tribal, not democratic. Its leaders were chieftains of extended families, rather than elected officials. So divisions of the army, encampment, and marching order were according to tribes, major tribal subunits, and families within them (Num. 1; 2). Likewise, the encampment and responsibilities of members of the tribe of Levi were according to their relationships as priests belonging to the family of Aaron, or as descendants of Kohath, Gershon, or Merari (Num. 3; 4).

Israelite extended families were to live, work, travel, and fight together in close cooperation. Since members were related, they understood each other and had a powerful vested interest in helping each other's well-being, safety, and success. In our individualistic, highly mobile, postagricultural modern Western societies, we have largely lost the strong sense of belonging, support, and identity that extended families can provide.

Israel was unified by a representative form of government. Leaders of smaller social units reported to leaders of larger units, who were under the guidance of Moses, the spokesperson for God, the divine king (cf. Num. 23:21). Moses was not elected, and neither was God. Representatives did not function as a parliament or congress to enact laws. Rather, they were responsible for seeing to it that the nation carried out the Lord's instructions. He was in charge.

So the Israelite government was a theocracy, ruled by God.

Rule by God

When you visit the capital city of a country, it is usually not difficult to find out who is in charge. The powers that be generally have their headquarters in a central location at an imposing capitol, parliament building, or palace. Abu Simbel in southern Egypt has an ancient picture of an Egyptian war camp, with the large tent of Pharaoh Ramses II (ruled 1279 to 1212 B.C.) in the middle. There was no question who had ultimate authority.

16

The pharaoh's tent was structured like the Israelite sanctuary, with a square inner room and an outer room twice that size. In the picture the royal cartouche (an oval-shaped "seal" representing the identity of the pharaoh) is in the middle of the inner "holy of holies." This is precisely equivalent to the location in the Israelite sanctuary where the Lord was enthroned above and between the cherubim on the ark of the covenant (Ex. 25:22; 1 Sam. 4:4; 2 Kings 19:15). Egypt claimed to have a theocracy, with pharaohs as god-kings. But the great Ramses II was just a human being, as you can see by observing his shriveled mummy in the museum at Cairo. It was Israel that had the real God-king.

Have you ever wondered what it would be like to have God as the head of state in your country? Not a faulty human president, prime minister, monarch, or dictator for life, but the Lord Himself? He would have the wisdom and power to solve all problems and would be totally fair (Ps. 96). God would rule by love, balancing justice and mercy (Ps. 85:10; 89:14). Special interests could not buy Him, and He would tolerate no corruption in His government. And He would never take a vacation or even go to sleep, but would constantly protect His people (Ps. 121:4). Who would not vote for such a leader?

God was the head of state of ancient Israel, and He communicated His will to Moses, His spokesman. "Now when Moses went into the tabernacle of meeting to speak with Him, he heard the voice of One speaking to him from above the mercy seat that was on the ark of the Testimony, from between the two cherubim; thus He spoke to him" (Num. 7:89). The content of such communication consisted of instructions for the Israelites (Ex. 25:22; Lev. 1:1, 2).

Moses was like God's prime minister in the sense that he was responsible for ensuring that the Lord's will got carried out and for arranging its details. But he was not in charge of formulating policy—that was the Lord's job. Israel's government was a theocracy, ruled by God.

In later ages, including modern times, many groups belonging to monotheistic religions (for example, the Taliban) have claimed to establish civil governments ruled by deity. But they are not true theocracies, because they have lacked the real presence of the Lord dwelling among them and directing them. They have tended to use claims of divine authority to force others to observe their human traditions. Often the results have been oppressive or even gruesome.

God's true Christian church on earth lacks both a civil government and the Shekinah presence of the Lord enthroned at the Holy of Holies of an earthly sanctuary or temple. We only have a community of faith. But the head of this community is the divine Christ (Eph. 5:23, 24), and the Holy Spirit continues to teach and to remind of Christ's teaching (John 14:26; 16:12-15).

So the true church must be a theocracy. Therefore, as in ancient Israel, the Lord's representatives are responsible for carrying out His will in His way. They are to apply divine principles, not to alter or replace them according to human reasoning. To do so would be to arrogantly and foolishly usurp the place of God, which would be blasphemy. Of course, they must work out and administer many practical details, but in doing so they should never disregard or compromise God's "blueprint" of principles that He has revealed through His prophetic spokespersons.

When the true church administers discipline to its members, it does so in harmony with God's will, as revealed through the Bible and the guidance of the Holy Spirit. Jesus said: "Truly I say to you, whatever you bind on earth shall have been bound in heaven; and whatever you loose on earth shall have been loosed in heaven" (Matt. 18:18, NASB). This translation, unlike a number of others, correctly renders the Greek tense, which means that the corporate body of believers makes decisions in harmony with what God has already decided. It does not mean that the church is in charge and heaven follows its will. We must humbly submit to the voice that speaks to us from between the heavenly cherubim.

Chapter 2

A HOLY PEOPLE
(Numbers 5; 6)

Divine Help to Regain Trust

A holy people consists of families. Families are united by marriages. Marriages are held together by trust. When trust breaks down in marriages, the fabric of society starts to unravel. In Western societies today we see this happening on a massive scale.

God gave Adam and Eve to each other in marriage as "one flesh" (Gen. 2), but maintaining such oneness can be a challenge in a fallen world. No sooner had Adam and Eve sinned than it damaged the trust between them. When God confronted them with what they had done, Adam blamed Eve (Gen. 3:12). Blaming each other has damaged marriages ever since.

It is extremely serious when one marriage partner accuses the other of being unfaithful by committing adultery. If such a claim is true, it justifies ending the marriage altogether (Matt. 5:32). Even if the claim is unfounded, suspicion destroys the basis on which the relationship rests. When it comes to the potential of private, intimate affairs, it can be hard for one spouse to know what is going on, or for the other person to explain.

God cares about the marriages of His people. Numbers 5:11–31 shows how He went to great lengths to help Israelite marriage partners overcome suspicion of marital infidelity, which could wreck their homes even if nobody had done anything wrong. However, several aspects of the passage seem strange and even offensive to a modern reader. Most disturbing is the fact that the Lord provided a procedure to address a man's suspicion of his wife, but no corresponding instruction regarding a suspected adulterous husband. This seems unfair, particularly because the ritual of the suspected adulterous wife sounds harsh and humiliating. The ritual is peculiar, especially the part in which the woman must drink water containing dust from the floor of the sanctuary (verses 17, 24).

To understand what God was trying to do, we must first remember that in Israelite society men basically had charge of legal matters. It does not mean that women were not important. Neither does it mean that we should exclude modern Christian women from the legal domain. The Lord was simply working with a group of people as they were. Men controlled the Israelite legal courts that judged claims of adultery. So an all-male court could easily be biased toward a husband. Consequently, a wife suspected of adultery could face the danger of being condemned to death, even if she had been faithful to her husband.

Innocent women accused of adultery needed special protection so that all-male courts could not lynch them. Men accused of adultery did not need such protection, so there was no ritual for a suspected male adulterer. It is true that the Israelite judicial system required at least two witnesses before it could impose capital punishment (Deut. 17:6; 19:15), and the male lover of an adulterous woman was to be executed with her (cf. Lev. 22:22). Such rules protected both men and women from unproven accusations. But a husband could be convinced in his own mind that his wife was fooling around, even if he could not prove it or identify the other man. The husband could be tempted to manufacture testimony against his wife, but even if he remained with her, the marriage would not be happy.

To protect suspected women and their marriages, God took their cases out of the hands of human courts and judged them Himself. It is the only kind of case that the Lord Himself decided at His sanctuary headquarters. He granted a "Supreme Court hearing" only to women.

God did not need an elaborate ritual to condemn or acquit

women suspected of adultery. He knew the real situation and could have easily communicated His verdicts more simply, such as through the priestly oracle of the Urim and Thummim (Ex. 28:30; Num. 27:21). But a solemn ceremony at the sanctuary would impress upon a suspicious husband that justice was fully served and that the Lord's verdict was right. If God condemned his wife, his suspicions would be confirmed, and she would be punished. However, if the Lord vindicated her as innocent, he could relax and accept her as faithful without hesitation. In this way their marriage could be healed.

To resolve the suspicion, a husband brings his wife to a priest at the Lord's sanctuary with a grain offering. His offering lacked oil or frankincense (Num. 5:15), unlike a normal grain offering (Lev. 2:1) for a happier occasion. The priest had the woman stand before the Lord, as her judge. She let down her hair as a sign of humility before God, and the priest placed the grain offering in her hands (Num. 5:16, 18). Then he made her take an oath, which was a conditional curse upon her if she had been unfaithful to her husband (verses 19-22). The priest wrote the curse and erased the words off into holy water (verse 23), into which he had mixed dust from the floor of the sanctuary (verse 17). It was a potent brew! Next, the priest offered the grain offering to the Lord, and finally he had her drink the water (verses 24-26).

When the liquid entered the body of the suspected adulterer, the presence or absence of punishment from God revealed the divine verdict. If she tested positive for guilt, her reproductive organs were damaged, and she became unable to bear any more children. If she was innocent, nothing happened to her, and she retained her fertility (verses 27, 28).

The procedure was a kind of litmus test—a no-pregnancy-in-the-future test. It was based on the principles that purity and holiness are compatible, but impurity and holiness are antagonistic. Compare Leviticus 7:20, 21, in which anyone who ate from a holy sacrifice while in a state of physical ritual impurity would suffer the-divine penalty of "cutting off," meaning that he or she would lose an afterlife (through a line of descendants, etc.). In Numbers 5 the testing substance was holy water. Dust from the floor of the sacred

21

sanctuary enhanced its holiness, and its testing function was emphasized by symbolically putting the conditional curse into it. A woman who was morally pure would have no problem coming into contact with the holy substance. But a guilty woman would suffer from the bad "chemical" reaction between her moral impurity and the Lord's holiness.

Without question the ritual of the suspected adulterous wife served as a deterrent to adultery. Even if there were no human witnesses, God saw everything and held people accountable. A woman who evaded punishment by a human court could nevertheless suffer profound physical discomfort, the sorrow of infertility (a major blow for a Hebrew woman), and a permanent stigma as glaring as a scarlet letter A for adultery (Num. 5:27). Conviction of a woman in this way often led to apprehending the male partner in crime.

On the other hand, a woman exonerated by God could continue life with her reputation untarnished and her marriage fully restored. This would be a remarkable blessing for her and her husband. In human life suspicion often drags on for lifetimes or even for multiple generations. Even when it is completely baseless, it tends to create a reality of its own, destroying everything it touches. But the Lord wanted to set His families free from suspicion so that they could be strong, united by trusting love.

For Israelites who were loyal to God, it was good that He knew everything about them. Nothing was hidden from Him. So the only sensible approach was to say with David: "Search me, God, and know my heart; try me, and know my anxieties; and see if there is any wicked way in me, and lead me in the way everlasting" (Ps. 139:23, 24). To those who love and trust the Lord, this is reassuring, not threatening. Even when David tragically committed adultery (2 Sam. 11), God was able to lead him to repentance and a higher level of moral purity (Ps. 51).

Hannah Senesh longed for an all-knowing friend. She was a young Jewish Hungarian resistance fighter in World War II caught by the Nazis, interrogated with torture, and finally shot by a firing squad. Hannah wrote the following poem in 1942 (translated from modern Hebrew):

Loneliness
"Could I meet one who understood all . . .
Without word, without search,
Confession or lie,
Without asking why.

"I would spread before him, like a white cloth,
The heart and the soul . . .
The filth and the gold.
Perceptive, he would understand.

"And after I had plundered the heart,
When all had been emptied and given away,
I would feel neither anguish nor pain,
But would know how rich I became."[1]

Another woman had such a friend. She had been a sinner, not merely suspected of sin. When she heard that the Lord was eating at the home of a Pharisee, she went to Him. Her husband did not take her there. Instead, she brought an offering to the Lord and let down her own hair to wash His feet humbly with her tears and wipe them with her hair.

Then the Pharisee mentally labeled her as the sinner she had been (Luke 7:37–39). The Lord knew everything she had done. And He also knew everything that the Pharisee had done. He even read his accusing thoughts and answered them, though the astonished Pharisee had said nothing out loud. The Lord did not judge the woman to be innocent, as He vindicated a blameless woman suspected of adultery in Numbers 5. Indeed she had been guilty. Rather, He said to her: "Your sins are forgiven" and "Your faith has saved you. Go in peace" (Luke 7:48, 50).

Special Holiness for Ordinary People

Only male Israelites descended from Aaron could come especially close to God by serving as consecrated priests at the sanctuary (Lev. 8). Most Israelites could never attain such a level of holiness.

Nevertheless, the Lord gave the opportunity for both men and women to enjoy another kind of special holiness for a period of time by taking the vow of a Nazirite. This vow showed exceptional devotion to the Lord by a lifestyle of abstinence and by offering a group of sacrifices (Num. 6). In this way the Lord affirmed that they belonged to "a kingdom of priests" and "a holy nation" (Ex. 19:6).

Many Christians regard their professional ministers as especially holy, even if they do not call them "Reverend" or "His Holiness" or regard them as priests. Indeed, professional ministry is a high and holy calling of spiritual leadership and exemplary life. But it is important to remember that all Christians are "a royal priesthood, a holy nation" (1 Peter 2:9). "According to Peter, all Christians belong to the priesthood. In the New Testament, the church does not have a priesthood—it is a priesthood."[2]

So all Christians, male or female, young or old, are ministers in a larger sense, even if they are not paid professional ministers. Our only priest in the special sense of a mediator with God is Christ (see especially Hebrews 7-10). So all Christians are to be holy: "as He who called you is holy, you also be holy in all your conduct, because it is written, 'Be holy, for I am holy'" (1 Peter 1:15, 16, citing Lev. 11:44). Even though it is no longer possible to fulfill a Nazirite vow (the sacrificial system is gone), the instructions to Nazirites show how God values and honors special devotion from men and women who are not professional ministers.

During the time of his or her vow, a Nazirite was to abstain from three things:

1. Foods and liquids made from grapes and from liquids made from similar sweet fruits susceptible to fermentation (Num. 6:3, 4).

2. Having a haircut (verse 5).

3. Approaching a dead body, even to bury closest relatives (verses 6, 7).

The first and third echoed prohibitions observed by priests. However, priests were forbidden to drink wine or another kind of (in this case fermented) drink from sweet fruit only when they entered the sanctuary (Lev. 10:9), and only the high priest could not participate in funerals of his closest relatives (Lev. 21:11; cf. verses 1-

4 for ordinary priests). The lifestyle of Nazirites, whose hair was dedicated to the Lord, was closest to that of the high priest, whose head was especially consecrated (Lev. 8:12; 21:10).

The culminating point of the Nazirite votive period came at the end, when the person offered a group of sacrifices. They included a purification offering, a burnt offering, and a well-being offering, along with a basket of unleavened grain items and accompanying grain and drink offerings (Num. 6:13-17, 19, 20). The combination of offerings was quite expensive (cf. Acts 21:24). With it the Nazirite would offer whatever else he or she had vowed, in accordance with what he or she could afford.

A Nazirite's sacrifices were similar in several ways to those by which Israel consecrated the priests: a purification offering, a burnt offering, and an ordination offering that was much like the well-being offering. With the ordination offering was a basket of unleavened grain items (Lev. 8). However, whereas the consecration rituals of the priests occurred at the beginning of their lifelong service to the Lord, a Nazirite's sacrifices came at the end of a temporary period of consecration.

As part of the concluding ceremony, the Nazirite would shave off his or her hair, which was dedicated to the Lord, and burn it on the fire under the well-being offering (Num. 6:18). Because the hair represented devotion of the whole person to God, offering it was as close as the Israelite ritual system came to human sacrifice. It pointed forward to the sacrifice of a dedicated human being: Christ, who vowed to offer Himself in order to take away sins:

"For it is not possible that the blood of bulls and goats could take away sins. Therefore, when He came into the world, He said: 'Sacrifice and offering You did not desire, but a body You have prepared for Me. In burnt offerings and sacrifices for sin You had no pleasure. Then I said, "Behold, I have come—in the volume of the book it is written of Me—to do Your will, O God"'" (Heb. 10:4-7, citing Ps. 40:6-8).

To promise His deliverance, Christ appeared to Manoah and his wife as the "Angel of the Lord" and gave them instructions for the lifelong Nazirite (Samson) she was to bear. He identified Himself as the one whose name is "Wonderful" (cf. Isa. 9:6). Then He ascended to heaven in the flame of a burnt offering, foreshadowing His offering of Himself (Judges 13:9-23).

Christ was from Nazareth, but He was not a Nazirite (Matt. 11:19). No linguistic connection exists between the two words, even though they sound similar in English. Therefore, it is highly unlikely that He had the long hair of a Nazirite that artists often depict. However, like a Nazirite, Christ offered His sacrifice at the end of His temporary, dedicated period of life on earth. This sacrifice qualified Him to become our permanent high priest in heaven, who "always lives to make intercession" for us (Heb. 7:25). So His sacrifice on the cross comes between His earthly life and His heavenly ministry.

When Nazirites had completed their offerings, they were free to drink wine again (Num. 6:20). But Jesus gave up this privilege, saying just before His death: "I will not drink of this fruit of the vine from now on until that day when I drink it new with you in My Father's kingdom" (Matt. 26:29). Until He can enjoy it with us, He will not enjoy it at all.

Blessing God's People

Israelite priests were a blessing to the people of God as His representatives by officiating at rituals, such as those of the pure or impure suspected adulterous wife (Num. 5:11-31) and the holy Nazirite (Num. 6:1-21). Priests as mediators for the people also blessed them by praying to invoke God on their behalf. Thus Aaron blessed the people at the end of the inaugural service (Lev. 9:22; cf. verse 23).

Blessing the people was so important that in Numbers 6:24-26 God Himself gave His priests the words to do it, just as Jesus presented His disciples with the Lord's Prayer as an example of how to pray (Matt. 6:9-13). The "priestly blessing" of Numbers 6, which we could regard as the "Lord's Prayer of the Old Testament," goes like this:

"May the Lord bless you
   and guard you;
May the Lord make His face shine toward you
   and be gracious to you;
May the Lord lift up His face toward you
   and give you well-being" (Num. 6:24-26, my translation).[3]

This brief, beautiful blessing is structured as poetry. Because it is spoken by a human being and asks God to bless His people, the prayer is a request (cf. Ps. 115:15; 134:3). The fact that the representative of the Lord pronounces it, using words that He has provided, provides assurance that God is ready and willing to answer. He invites petition to Him: "Ask, and it will be given to you; seek, and you will find; knock, and it will be opened to you" (Matt. 7:7). God's people do not need to be timid about asking for benefits, because the King of the universe Himself has urged them to come boldly to His throne of grace (Heb. 4:16). God loves His people and is eager to lavish upon them the benefits of His good favor, including protection and well-being. They do not have to earn His favor—they only need to accept it.

The priestly blessing refers to the Lord's face shining toward His people and being lifted up toward them. Both images express His positive attitude of gracious goodwill toward them, from which all blessings flow. They do not have to strive for each benefit one by one. They just need to focus on the one who provides everything, as Jesus said: "But seek first the kingdom of God and His righteousness, and all these things shall be added to you" (Matt. 6:33).

Numbers 6:27 says that when the priests would bless the Israelites, "they shall put My name on the children of Israel, and I will bless them." Assurance of blessing comes from possessing God's "name." Those who have His name belong to Him as His holy people. He provides their identity, and they are under His care.

The Lord's name also represents His character and reputation (Ex. 9:16; Eze. 36:23). So bearing His name is both a privilege and a responsibility. Everything we are and do is connected with His name. By allowing Him to work in and through us, we permit Him to glorify His name in the world so that others will be drawn to Him. On the other hand, if we claim His name but fail to cooperate with the outworking of His grace in our lives, we take His name in vain (Ex. 20:7).

God's favor and goodwill are available to all inhabitants of Planet Earth through the gift of His Son. When Jesus was born, the angels sang: "Glory to God in the highest, and on earth peace, goodwill toward men!" (Luke 2:14). By being lifted up on the cross to make provision for the salvation of all who will accept His grace, Christ invites all peoples to come to Him (John 12:32). He is the priest of everyone, not only of the Israelites, and His blessing is ready for them. Whatever their name may have been in the past, He has a new name to put on them, a new identity and character signifying that they belong to God for all time (Rev. 3:12).

---

[1] Translated from the Hebrew by Ruth Finer Mintz, in *Hannah Senesh: Her Life and Diary* (New York: Schocken Books, 1971), p. 253.

[2] Russell Burrill, *Revolution in the Church* (Fallbrook, Calif.: Hart Research Center, 1979), p. 24.

[3] Roy Gane, *Leviticus, Numbers, NIV Application Commentary* (Grand Rapids: Zondervan, 2004), p. 539.

Chapter 3

SERVING GOD

(Numbers 7; 8)

Gifts for Service to God

One fine Sabbath day during the summer, my family went to a picnic area by a small lake in southwestern Michigan. With us were my wife's parents and some friends of our teenage daughter. Spreading a cloth on the picnic table, we laid out the food. There was plenty to eat. But to our profound chagrin, we discovered that we had forgotten to pack silverware. When we tried to eat beans and potato salad with potato chips, the chips kept breaking in midair before we could get the food into our eager mouths. Someone suggested eating with twigs from a nearby tree, but we were not used to eating with chopsticks. We were getting more frustrated by the minute. Starvation seemed imminent, and we were in danger of coveting the silverware of other picnickers.

When the chips are down, you ask for help. So my wife went over to another group of people, who were enjoying their food in a civilized manner, and sheepishly asked if we could borrow any extra utensils they might have. They had some and kindly agreed. In fact, they were so kind that they refrained from laughing at us. We proceeded to eat our lunch and soon recovered from embarrassment and hunger.

When you are carrying out an activity with a group of people, you need the necessary supplies and tools. This was true for the Israelites responsible for worship activities at the sanctuary. What would be offered on the altar on behalf of all Israel, including every morning and evening (Ex. 29:38-42)? How would the priests collect the blood from the sacrificial animals, and what containers would they use for drink offerings? What would carry the portable sanctuary when it needed to be moved? Numbers 7 answers these questions by listing gifts that the chieftains representing the 12 tribes of Israel gave to the Lord's sanctuary, including the altar, when it was consecrated.

Leviticus 8 describes the consecration ceremony earlier. But Numbers 7 records the gifts, probably because they have to do with equipment and supplies for the sanctuary rather than ritual performance. Equipment and supplies were important in order to provide for the activities of the sanctuary.

The first set of gifts from the chiefs consisted of six covered wagons and two oxen to pull each wagon. The two divisions of Levites (descended from Gershon and Merari) needed them to transport the disassembled sanctuary from place to place. However, the Kohathite Levites did not receive wagons, because they were to carry items of furniture and utensils on their shoulders (Num. 7:2-9; cf. Num. 4).

Transporting sacred objects on shoulders would protect these items from jostling about in a wagon. Remember that ancient vehicles lacked rubber tires and soft suspension, and roads were not smooth. It is unfortunate that when David first tried to transfer the ark of the covenant to Jerusalem he had it hauled on a wagon, rather than properly carried on long poles over the shoulders of priests (cf. Deut. 31:9; Joshua 3:3, 6, 8, etc.). When the oxen pulling the wagon made it unsteady, Uzzah grasped the ark in order to keep it in place, but the Lord struck him dead (2 Sam. 6:3-7). The Lord had commanded that none but the priests were to touch the ark, and so the intense holiness of it was simply off-limits to him, just as high-voltage electricity or nuclear radiation is to anyone not properly protected.

The second set of gifts from the Israelite chieftains on behalf of their tribes was for the dedication of the altar. The supplies for the sacred activities connected with the altar included silver and gold bowls and pans (including ones for drink offerings and collecting blood), materials for grain offerings, incense, and animals for public sacrifices on behalf of the whole nation (cf. Num. 28; 29).

Apparently to give due recognition to the gifts from each tribe and to prolong the celebration, each chieftain made his contribution on a subsequent day during a 12-day period (Num. 7:10-88).

The gifts from the 12 tribes were impressive and expensive (verses 84-88). They must have received many of these things, as well as the materials for building the sanctuary (Ex. 35), from the Egyptians (Ex. 12:35, 36) as partial compensation for the forced Israelite labor from which Egypt had profited (Ex. 1; 2; 5).

Why would the Lord want such wealth, earned by the sweat of slaves, to be lavished upon His sanctuary and its altar? Would it not have been better to give all this to the poor? Jesus answered that kind of question when a woman anointed His head with very costly oil.

"But when His disciples saw it, they were indignant, saying, 'Why this waste? For this fragrant oil might have been sold for much and given to the poor.' But when Jesus was aware of it, He said to them, 'Why do you trouble the woman? For she has done a good work for Me. For you have the poor with you always, but Me you do not have always.

" 'For in pouring this fragrant oil on My body, she did it for My burial. Assuredly, I say to you, wherever this gospel is preached in the whole world, what this woman has done will also be told as a memorial to her' " (Matt. 26:8-13).

Giving directly to the Lord does not replace an obligation to help the poor (Lev. 25:35).

But He deserves special honor, the best that His people have available. Anything they offer to Him is a mere token, returning a tiny portion of all that He has granted to them. By honoring Him, they direct the attention of others to His greatness.

The woman honored Jesus in a way that pointed forward to His sacrifice. So did the Israelite sanctuary and its sacrifices at the altar.

The Israelites concentrated their worship resources toward a single sanctuary or Temple, in which they conducted sacrifices and other rituals. Today we have many churches for prayer, praise, and teaching and preaching from God's Word. While our churches are also places of worship, they are not the same as the ancient sanctuary/Temple. So we cannot and should not make extremely expensive churches. But God deserves the best that we can reasonably provide. Now that Christ has already accomplished His sacrifice, He is all the more worthy of honor.

Let Your Light Shine—in the Right Direction

Light is a necessity for many human activities, not merely a luxury. Years ago a college student told me that her mother and father had been flying trapeze artists at a circus. In one of their stunt routines the mother was to let go of her swing and fly through the air to her husband, who would catch her by the hands. All this took place high in the air, without a safety net below.

But on one occasion, at the precise moment when the woman had released her hold on the swing, the lights suddenly went out. It was pitch-dark, and she could not see anything. Hurtling through the air, she missed her husband and happened to run into one of the main posts that supported the huge circus tent. With the lightning reflexes of a professional acrobat, she threw her arms around the post and slid all the way to the ground below. The instant she reached the bottom, the lights flashed back on. The crowd wildly cheered and applauded. Thinking the incredible feat was arranged, they wanted her to do it again! However, she was fortunate to be alive, and never intentionally tried that trick without light.

When the army of Pharaoh trapped the Israelites by the Red Sea, light from the Lord helped the Israelites. But darkness from Him prevented the Egyptians from attacking His people. "And the Angel of God, who went before the camp of Israel, moved and went behind them; and the pillar of cloud went from before them and stood behind them. So it came between the camp of the Egyptians and the camp of Israel. Thus it was a cloud and darkness to the one, and it gave light by night to the other, so that the one did not come near the other all that night (Ex. 14:19, 20).

It was not the only time that the Lord's glory cloud provided light and the assurance of protection for His people. Every night His cloud changed to the appearance of fire and rested over His sanctuary (Ex. 13:21; Num. 9:15, 16, 21). No enemy could approach under cover of darkness, and the unearthly glow hovering in the air would intimidate anyone thinking of molesting them. Unlike modern security lights, the Lord's light was 100 percent reliable because the power never went out.

Another light glowed in the outer "living room" of the sanctuary, but human beings ignited it. A priest was responsible for trimming the lamps on the lampstand every morning and lighting them every evening so that they would burn throughout the night (Ex. 27:21; 30:8). The Lord's light was always on because "the guardian of Israel neither slumbers nor sleeps!" (Ps. 121:4, Tanakh).

Having a light is not enough. It must be allowed to shine in the right direction to provide useful illumination. So the Lord instructed Aaron: "When you arrange the lamps, the seven lamps shall give light in front of the lampstand" (Num. 8:2; cf. Ex. 25:37). That is, the lamps should be pointed toward the center of the outer apartment of the sanctuary in order to illuminate that whole area.

Jesus also talked about letting light from our lives go out where it can do its job:

"You are the light of the world. A city that is set on a hill cannot be hidden. Nor do they light a lamp and put it under a basket, but on a lampstand, and it gives light to all who are in the house. Let your light so shine before men, that they may see your good works and glorify your Father in heaven" (Matt. 5:14-16).

Our light comes from God and should be reflected back toward Him. The point is to draw attention to the Lord, to whom all glory is due, rather than to ourselves. When others recognize and accept God as their source of light, they will not stumble or fly through the darkness.

Qualifying Workers

The Israelite priests came from the tribe of Levi, and other men from the same tribe were to assist them in taking care of the sanctuary. The other Levites were not consecrated as priests, but they had to be purified and set apart from the rest of the Israelites so that they could safely come into close proximity to holy things in order to perform their duties (Num. 8:5-22). Their purification freed them from physical ritual impurity, especially of corpse contamination.

Such defilement had affected them at various times in the past, as when they participated in funerals. But they had had no means or reason to be cleansed until now.

Physical ritual impurity involves a kind of thinking very foreign to us. Or is it? When I was 9 years old, my male classmates at an elementary school in Lincoln, Nebraska, avoided touching things that belonged to or had been handled by girls. Members of the female species were supposed to convey a kind of contagion called "cooties," which was a threat to developing masculinity. Avoiding "cooties" and shrilly warning one another about them was an entertaining game. Of course, "cooties" did not survive our puberty, when deadly hormones killed our desire to stay away from "cuties."

Only in adulthood did I learn that the word "cooties" literally means "lice." I do not imagine for a moment that the lovely young women of fourth grade were infested with even a single louse. For the boys, "cooties" was a conceptual category that symbolized a transferable quality of femininity. Undoubtedly specialists in human developmental psychology would be able to explain this kind of thinking, which seems to represent a rather insecure stage at which a boy needs to affirm his gender. But for our purposes it is enough to point out that the "cooties" category involved a human physical source (a girl) and things especially associated with her by ownership or touch. We boys regarded it as a kind of "impurity" that we needed to avoid.

"Cooties" provide a rather trivial example that can help us understand the profound biblical concept of human physical ritual impurity. Such impurity did not result from ordinary dirt. Nor was it disease, although some diseases could make people impure. Nor was it sin in the sense of breaking a divine command. Rather, Israelite impurity was a conceptual category associated with the birth-to-death cycle of mortality that has resulted from sin (Gen. 3; Rom. 5:12; 6:23). So impurities emphasizing mortality could come from dead bodies (Num. 19), the living death of a disease-causing deterioration of the skin (Lev. 13; 14; Num. 12), and male and female flows of various kinds from reproductive organs, which were for generating new mortal life (Lev. 15). Even though birth brought forth new life, it was mortal life, and so the mother's postpartum flow of blood made her impure (Lev. 12).

Whoever or whatever was "impure" was not permitted to come in contact with holy things or places. So rather than dividing "male" from "female," physical ritual impurity separated "divine" from "fallen human." Having an impurity did not mean that an Israelite was worth less than other people. Indeed, it was good to become impure in order to enjoy the intimacy of marriage and continue the human race by receiving the divine blessing to "be fruitful and multiply" (Gen. 1:28; 9:1). It was also necessary to become impure by burying one's parents in partial fulfillment of the command, "Honor your father and your mother" (Ex. 20:12).

We can call this "ritual impurity" because the holiness from which it needed to be kept was the holiness of the sanctuary and its ritual system, in which the divine presence resided on earth. Such division was no trivial matter. Summarizing a series of instructions regarding ritual impurities and purification from them, God warned: "Thus you shall separate the children of Israel from their uncleanness, lest they die in their uncleanness when they defile My tabernacle that is among them" (Lev. 15:31). Because the Israelite camp contained the sanctuary, it was holy. That was why seriously impure persons had to stay outside the camp (Num. 5:1-4).

The God of Israel insisted on distancing Himself from mortality. Death was never part of the original divine plan, contrary to human philosophies going all the way back to ancient Egypt. In Egypt every tomb was a temple because death was the holy passage to the next phase of immortal life with the gods. But what we need is redemption from death, not merely reincarnation (or reincarceration?) to another state.

The holy God of Israel is the Lord of life (Matt. 22:32). He rejects the idea that death is holy and therefore associated with Himself. In the Bible a dead human body was impure and therefore excluded from contact with holy things or holy people (Lev. 21:10-12; Num. 6:6-9; 19:11-22). Death is evil, the result of sin (Gen. 3; Rom. 6:23). God wants to restore eternal life to us (John 3:16), not to merely perpetuate an "immortal soul," which is a fictitious notion invented by His enemy (Gen. 3:4).

Now the Israelite sanctuary and Temple are gone. Christ's ministry is in the better sanctuary in heaven (Heb. 7-10). God's Shekinah presence no longer resides at an earthly dwelling. So there is no holy place on earth in the sense that the Israelite sanctuary and surrounding camp were holy. Therefore we do not need to fight in order to gain or maintain control over holy territory by any means possible in order to carry out rituals at a place designated for special access to God. What a relief! Neither do we have to observe the biblical laws regarding physical ritual impurity in order to separate such impurity from an earthly sphere of holiness.

Some well-meaning Christians are trying to resurrect purity laws as mandatory requirements, including treating women differently during certain times of the month, but they are misguided and imposing unnecessary burdens and confusion. They are also inconsistent, picking and choosing laws without adequately recognizing that they belong to a system the Israelites had to observe as a whole.

Nobody, whether Jew or Christian, can possibly keep the system of ritual impurity and purification laws in the proper manner today, because this system requires purifying sacrifices at a functioning sanctuary/Temple (Lev. 12:6-8; 14:10-20, etc.), something that no longer exists. Without the ashes of the red heifer to purify everyone from corpse contamination (Num. 19), all are simply impure, as the Levites were before their purification rituals (Num. 8). But for us this does not matter, as it did not matter for the Levites before the establishment of the sanctuary.

Although we do not need to keep the purity laws, they can teach us about human nature in relation to divine nature and the way that God heals us from mortality in addition to forgiving our sins (Ps. 103:3). Sacrifices to purify Israelites from serious physical ritual impurities pointed forward to Christ's sacrifice, as did sacrifices for sins. They teach us that Christ died not only to forgive us our sinful actions, but also to deliver us from our underlying mortal state of sin. Jesus said to Nicodemus: "For God so loved the world that He gave His only begotten Son, that whoever believes in Him should not perish but have everlasting life" (John 3:16). As a result, when Christ comes again, He will change the mortality of all who accept Him into immortality (1 Cor. 15:51-54).

Purifying the Levites from physical ritual impurity involved sprinkling "water of purification" on them, which removed corpse contamination (see Num. 19), and having them shave their whole bodies and wash their clothes. In addition, a purification offering and burnt offering were to be performed on their behalf (Num. 8:6-8, 12, 21). The purpose of the pair of sacrifices was to purify them (verse 21). So their purification occurred through water and blood sacrifice, foreshadowing the sacrifice of Christ, "who came by water and blood" (1 John 5:6).

It is not mere coincidence that when Christ died and a soldier pierced His side with a spear, "blood and water came out" (John 19:34). Nor is it accidental that Jesus' first miracle involved turning water for purification into wine, which can represent blood (John 2:6-11; cf. Matt. 26:27, 28). Water and blood were the most important purifying agents of the Israelite ritual system, and the source of ultimate purification is Christ.

Purifying the Levites made it possible for them to carry out their sacred duties. Such work was on behalf of all the other Israelites, in place of their firstborn, as their representatives (Num. 8:16-18). To set the Levites apart in this way, the Israelites were to lay their hands on them (verse 10), as an offerer would lay a hand upon the head of a sacrificial animal (Lev. 1:4). Then Aaron, the high priest, performed a symbolic gesture (literally "raise as a raised offering") to dedicate the Levites to the Lord (Num. 8:11, 13, 21).

In a sense the Levites were a sacrificial gift presented by the people to the Lord, who gave them to the priests (cf. Lev. 7:34) to assist them with the work of the sanctuary. Thus the Levites were a kind of "living sacrifice." A "sacrifice" is something or someone given over to the holy realm of God for His use. Although it was necessary for Christ to die as the Sacrifice to save us from sin and death, His people can be "sacrifices" dedicated to God, without dying. Paul appealed to Christians:

"I beseech you therefore, brethren, by the mercies of God, that you present your bodies a living sacrifice, holy, acceptable to God, which is your reasonable service. And do not be conformed to this world, but be transformed by the renewing of your mind, that you

37

may prove what is that good and acceptable and perfect will of God" (Rom. 12:1, 2).

Like the ancient Levites, we can be living sacrifices dedicated to God to assist the gospel work of our High Priest, Jesus Christ. He does not need us to take care of utensils or to carry sacred objects from place to place. But He does want us to invite others to come to Him at the temple in heaven by faith, an invitation presented in the book of Hebrews: "Therefore, brethren, having boldness to enter the Holiest by the blood of Jesus, by a new and living way which He consecrated for us, through the veil, that is, His flesh, and having a High Priest over the house of God, let us draw near with a true heart in full assurance of faith, having our hearts sprinkled from an evil conscience and our bodies washed with pure water" (Heb. 10:19-22).

Chapter 4

GETTING READY TO MOVE
(Numbers 9; 10)

Independence Day

Many nations celebrate their independence from foreign rule with holidays. The dates vary, but the theme is similar: the joy of victory that has brought the opportunity for self-determination and freedom from exploitation. People look forward to such holidays as happy times to eat and drink with friends and family, watch parades, or listen to patriotic music and speeches. As a boy I especially enjoyed fireworks on Independence Day. Watching public fireworks displays was exciting, but even more thrilling was to light our own firecrackers and bottle rockets.

Passover is "independence day" for Israel, commemorating its deliverance from Egyptian oppression and the birth of the nation. People of many lands have believed that God aided their struggles for liberation, but the Israelites' story of divine, miraculous intervention on behalf of their nation of slaves is unique. So Israel's independence day is a religious festival to celebrate with God.

Shortly before the Israelites departed from the Wilderness of Sinai, they enjoyed their second Passover. It was their first celebration of it outside Egypt. A year before, they had observed Passover just before their God actually accomplished their final deliverance (Ex. 12). That "independence day" celebration was an act of faith that God was about to set them free.

Later in the Bible we again see this pattern of faith celebration, anticipating what God was about to do. When the Israelites marched around Jericho seven times, priests blew trumpets and the people shouted. Then the walls fell down (Joshua 6:20). As a small child I imagined that the powerful noise cracked the walls of the city, so that they toppled. It is true that a high decibel level can rattle things and make them break. But having seen ancient Near Eastern city walls at archaeological sites, I no longer believe that the sound accomplished the job at Jericho. God did it. It was a miracle. All the Israelites did was to celebrate what He was about to do.

Interestingly, the same Hebrew word for the Israelites' "shout" (verse 20) appears in Numbers 23:21, in which Balaam gazed down on the Israelite camp and observed that "the shout of a King is among them." It was the acclamation of the Lord as the divine king of the Israelites. At Jericho they shouted to celebrate just that.

Centuries later, when a great multitude of enemies marched against Judah's King Jehoshaphat, he led his people in fasting and seeking help from the Lord (2 Chron. 20:1-13).

Then the Spirit of the Lord came upon Jahaziel, who gave the people a message from the Lord, including the injunction: "Do not be afraid nor dismayed because of this great multitude, for the battle is not yours, but God's" (verse 15). Jehoshaphat accepted the promise and worshipped the Lord, and Levites stood up to praise the Lord with loud voices (verses 18, 19). Celebration had already begun!

The next day, Jehoshaphat encouraged his people: "Believe in the Lord your God, and you shall be established; believe His prophets, and you shall prosper" (verse 20). It is crucial to believe God's promises, delivered through His prophets, in order to accept God's salvation through faith on the basis of His Word, as though it is already accomplished.

To confirm his words of faith, Jehoshaphat did something remarkable: "And when he had consulted with the people, he appointed those who should sing to the Lord, and who should praise the beauty of holiness, as they went out before the army and were saying: 'Praise the Lord, for His mercy endures forever' " (verse 21). Against that kind of faith, the enemies of God's people didn't stand a chance. The Lord set them against each other, so that they destroyed themselves. The army of Judah didn't need to fight at all (verses 22-24).

The same pattern of anticipation by faith continues into the New Testament. At the Last Supper Jesus observed Passover with His disciples and transformed it into a celebration of deliverance from the oppressive rule of Satan, who is far more powerful and dangerous than Pharaoh ever was (Matt. 26:17-30). Their celebration of independence from the evil "ruler of this world" (cf. John 12:31) rested on Christ's sacrifice (Matt. 26:26-28), which was about to take place (Matt. 27).

The first Passover and the first Lord's Supper came before the deliverances they celebrated. But then God's people were to observe them regularly in order to commemorate the salvation events after their completion. While these services involved remembering past experiences of receiving God's grace through faith, they also called for looking forward by faith to salvation's future culmination. Since the Lord had set the Israelites free from Egypt, they could trust that He would complete His promises by bringing them safely to their new home in the Promised Land. Similarly, the fact that the crucified Christ shattered Satan's right to Planet Earth (John 12:31) provides strong evidence for our faith in His future return to claim what belongs to Him and make all things new (Rev. 19-22).

As we see what God has already done for us, we have confidence in what He has promised. And it applies even at the level of individual experience. When we feel overwhelmed by powerful problems, forces, or temptations that seem about to destroy our lives, it is time to remember the humanly impossible odds that the Lord has easily overcome for His people in the past. We can claim His promises, as Jehoshaphat and his people did, and celebrate their imminent fulfillment. Even if God does not intervene in this life, as He chose not to rescue John the Baptist (Matt. 14:3-12), permanent deliverance is coming soon in the next life (cf. Job 19:25-27).

The Israelites were about to set forth from the safety and relative ease of camping by Mount Sinai to rugged travel and encounters with powerful enemies. Observing Passover to praise God for the way He had saved them from Pharaoh would reinforce their faith in what He was about to do for them so that they would courageously cooperate with Him. Praise strengthens faith, which provides courage.

The Israelites celebrated their second Passover at its appointed time on the fourteenth day of the first month, which was in the spring (Num. 9:1-5; cf. Ex. 12). This was "in the first month of the second year after they had come out of the land of Egypt" (Num. 9:1). Notice that this was a couple weeks before the Lord commanded Moses to carry out the military census "on the first day of the second month, in the second year after they had come out of the land of Egypt" (Num. 1:1). Here the organization of the account in the book of Numbers is thematic, rather than a strictly chronological report of events in the order they occurred. By recounting the Passover exercise of faith in Numbers 9, shortly before the notice of leaving Sinai (Num. 10:11-13), the book implies a parallel with the departure from Egypt a year before. The people were continuing their journey of faith with God.

At Passover, before beginning their rigorous march to Canaan, some Israelites had a problem. But their complaint was not faithlessness. Rather, they had wanted to enjoy the Passover celebration and were disappointed because the impurity of corpse contamination had prevented them from participating (Num. 9:6, 7).

Passover included eating holy sacrificial meat at home (Ex. 12). But anyone who had come into close proximity with a dead body became ritually impure for a week (Num. 19:11).

Consequently, they were not permitted to eat sacred food (cf. Lev. 7:20, 21) and had to remain outside the camp during their time of impurity, away from their homes (Num. 5:1-4).

Such rules had not been in effect a year earlier at the time of the first Passover, because the sanctuary, where the Lord's presence now dwelt in their midst, did not yet exist.

Now some people found themselves excluded from Passover by circumstances beyond their control. Their relatives had died, and they had had to bury them. Death cannot be scheduled. So in addition to grieving for their loved ones, they felt shut out of the community. The Lord sympathized with their concern, which He recognized as valid. So He established a second Passover date a month later on the fourteenth day of the second month for anyone who had incurred corpse contamination. He added the same provision for anyone on a distant journey, who was unable to make it home for the festival in the first month (Num. 9:9-12).

In Numbers 9 we see the character of God at work. His solution was practical and showed flexibility in order to include as many as possible in a special occasion of community rejoicing. He also included resident aliens who wished to observe the Israelite national independence festival of Passover. God treated such people the same as if they were Israelite citizens (verse 14; cf. Ex. 12:48, 49). In this way the Lord included foreigners of faith who identified with His chosen people, through whom He promised to bless all nations (Gen. 12:3; 22:18).

It would be wonderful if God's people would learn from Him how to treat others. We would then respect the feelings and valid limitations of other people, keep rules and their purpose in balanced perspective, and include as many as we could in our worship and celebration of salvation!

Staying Together

When my parents and brother and I moved from Nebraska to California in 1974, we took Interstate 80. My brother, 16 years old and unhappy about the move, preferred to drive alone in his old but rather classy brown Cadillac. The rest of us rode in a Plymouth that looked like a big blue box. The Cadillac had cruise control. The Plymouth did not.

So aside from the frustration of leaving his friends farther behind with every mile, my brother had to deal with the irritation of staying with another vehicle that kept speeding up and slowing down.

Whether you are driving, jogging, or working on a project, it is hard to go at someone else's pace. Either they move too fast or too slowly, too evenly or too bumpily, stop too frequently or not often enough. But if they are supporting, guiding, or protecting you, it pays to adjust and stay with them.

The Israelites needed to travel with God. It was a matter of survival. So after keeping the first Passover, when the Israelites departed from Egypt, "the Lord went before them by day in a pillar of cloud to lead the way, and by night in a pillar of fire to give them light, so as to go by day and night" (Ex. 13:21). When the Egyptian army pursued the Israelites, the Lord's cloud separated them from their former captives (Ex. 14:19, 20). During World War II ships would put out smoke screens to prevent enemy aircraft from seeing them. But the Lord's "smoke screen" was better because it simultaneously gave light to His people and darkness to their enemies.

Later the Lord's presence rested on Mount Sinai in a cloud that shielded the Israelites from His glory (Ex. 19:16; 24:15, 16, 18). However, after they constructed the sanctuary, the Lord's glory filled it, and His cloud moved into a position above it. The cloud stayed there until it was time to pull up stakes and journey onward (Ex. 40:34-38).

After reporting the second Passover, the book of Numbers reminds us of the Lord's glory cloud (Num. 9:15-23). This passage emphasizes that the Israelites followed the movements of that cloud, no matter how long or short the time it hovered over the sanctuary: "At the command of the Lord they remained encamped, and at the command of the Lord they journeyed; they kept the charge of the Lord, at the command of the Lord by the hand of Moses" (verse 23).

It is true that God set the pace, but the reality is that it was for the benefit of His people.

He could have gone to Canaan many times faster. But they were not ready. Their faith in and cooperation with Him needed to graduate from "boot camp" (or "sandal camp") before they were ready to face intimidating enemies. If the Lord's leading sometimes didn't make sense, it was to teach them to trust and follow Him at all times. He knew what He was doing.

Thus it was not enough for the Israelites to be where the Lord had been in the past or would likely be in the future. They needed to be where He was at that moment.

Unfortunately, many religious groups throughout the centuries have enshrined places or beliefs representing where they think the Lord was at one time. Tragically, they are not open for Him to lead them to new truth, because they resolutely cling to their mummified orthodoxy. They are focused on God, not as a person, but as an idea confined to a box that they have created. Adorning the box, they kiss it and periodically parade it around, but it is really a kind of coffin, and the living God is not inside.

Others are impatient with God's direction in the present. Because He is trying to keep a diverse flock together, He is too slow for them. They are the elite, out in front, leading the way, shattering paradigms.

But we are safe only if we are with God where He is now. We need to move with Him and pause with Him. Yes, He can go much faster, but He knows what is best for us.

Signals for Coordination

To coordinate a group of people, it is helpful to have signals. In the small town of Angwin, California, where I lived for several years, the excellent volunteer fire department uses a system of loud siren alarms to summon those needed to handle different kinds of emergencies. The more alarms that sound, the greater the emergency. Five alarms are for something major, such as a dangerous fire, requiring the rapid deployment of all members. When that happens, many workers rush from their jobs and leap into their vehicles, and their tires screech as they roar off. This energetic, well-trained, and dedicated force has saved many lives and homes.

Before the Israelites set out from Sinai to Canaan, they needed a system of signals to coordinate their movements rapidly and effectively. If they should assemble in order to receive instructions, or set out on another stage of their journey, or meet a threat from an enemy, passing the message by word of mouth would be far too slow. Remember that they had no loudspeakers, cell phones, or pagers. Without proper coordination, chaos would ensue. Members of the tribes of Judah, Issachar, Zebulun, etc., would be going this way and that, bumping into each other and shouting in frustration. If they had to move their animals as well, flocks and herds would collide and get mixed up, which would anger their owners. A cacophony of bleating, braying, and mooing would complete the mass confusion.

The Lord wants order that contributes to the accomplishment of His purposes. He is "not the author of confusion but of peace"

(1 Cor. 14:33). So He directed Moses to have two silver trumpets made, which priests would blow in certain ways (one or two trumpets, with different kinds of blasts), depending on what needed to happen (Num. 10:1–10). Now that archaeologists have found an ancient Egyptian silver trumpet in beautiful condition, we have an idea of what such an instrument could look like. With the piercing sound of these trumpets, it would be easy to get the attention of the Israelites in order to summon all of them (or only representative leaders), control the beginning of a march so that tribes would set out in the right order, declare war, or celebrate times of joy.

The fact that priests blew the trumpets reinforced the fact that the signals represented the Lord's will. The priests worked at the sanctuary, where they would receive directions from Him through Moses or by observing the movement of God's glory cloud. Then they would signal announcements to the people.

God told the Israelites that if enemies should afflict them, the trumpet alarm sounded by the priests would serve as a kind of prayer to their divine King, "and you will be remembered before the Lord your God, and you will be saved from your enemies" (Num. 10:9). Later leaders, who were not priests, also blew trumpets (but ram's horns) to gather Israelites to battle in which God gave them victory (see, for example, Judges 3:27; 6:34).

The priestly silver trumpets had another function: to cause the Israelites to be remembered before God at times of joy. "Also in the day of your gladness, in your appointed feasts, and at the beginning of your months, you shall blow the trumpets over your burnt offerings and over the sacrifices of your peace offerings; and they shall be a memorial for you before your God: I am the Lord your God" (Num. 10:10). The need for such remembrance did not mean that God had forgotten them. Rather, such trumpet blasts were prayers at special times to acknowledge their dependence upon Him and praise Him.

My family and I were walking on a trail toward a beach on Lake Michigan. All of a sudden we heard a powerful siren. This made us nervous, because we were a short distance from the Cook Nuclear Power Plant, which is naturally a potential target for terrorists. We asked some other hikers if they knew what was going on, and they said that it was a test alarm that sounded at that time once per month. Needless to say, we were relieved.

The Israelites also had regular signals at scheduled times, including at the beginning of each month, but one could distinguish their sound from emergency alarms. However, there was one exception: The remembrance (before the Lord) of trumpet blasts at the beginning of the seventh month (the "Feast of Trumpets"; Lev. 23:24) was the same as the summons for war (Num. 10:9). This was an annual reminder that their leader was a King (acclaimed with the same sound in Numbers 23:21) who was mighty and ready to help His people.

Blasts from the Israelite trumpets evoked a wide range of emotions, including curiosity regarding the reason for a divine summons, excitement of setting out to see new places along the way to the Promised Land, concern and adrenaline rush when facing the prospect of battle, and the exhilaration of celebrating the covenant with the Lord as one of His chosen people. The common element in all of this was the focus on God, who led, protected, and provided for them in all their circumstances.

Later in the history of God's people, prophets called on them to proclaim times of emergency and repentance with (ram's horn) trumpets (Isa. 58:1; Joel 2:1, 15). Similarly, when we have serious problems, we should acknowledge and confront them. A crisis is a crisis, whether leaders and their people admit it or not. Rather than hiding in apathy and a state of denial, pretending that everything is OK to protect our position and image, we should summon all parties involved, honestly seek God together, fully admit our mistakes, and claim the Lord's promises of forgiveness (1 John 1:9) and assistance (for example, James 1:5—promise of wisdom).

The Israelite trumpets are long gone, but in the book of Revelation an angel sounding a seventh trumpet announces God's kingship and consequently His judgment, and the ark of the covenant in His heavenly temple comes into view (Rev. 11:15-19). This is the end-time equivalent of the trumpet memorial at the beginning of the seventh month (Lev. 23:23-25), followed by the Day of Atonement judgment of loyalty to God (verses 26-32), when the high priest saw the Israelite ark of the covenant (Lev. 16). Another trumpet, the last one, will summon God's true people, not to a sanctuary in a wilderness camp, but from the grave to enjoy eternal life with His unveiled presence in the perpetual peace of paradise (1 Cor. 15:52; 1 Thess. 4:16; cf. Matt. 24:31).

Hitting the Road

Getting ready for a major trip is always a lot of work for my family. It is the case even if the house is already tidy, clothes are washed and folded, bills are paid, documents on computers are backed up, the oil in the van has been changed recently and the tires are properly inflated, there is plenty of food for the dogs and cats, and arrangements have been made for someone to take care of the animals. Usually we are tending to many or all of these things at the last minute, along with a never-ending stream of e-mail, plus university tasks that cannot wait until we get back (grading written assignments, turning in grades, advising students). Add a publication deadline for an article or book, and we have little or no time for sleep. When we finally get in our vehicle, pull out of the driveway, and hit the road, we share an overwhelming sense of relief and anticipation.

The Israelites had been getting ready for this moment for almost a year. It took a while, because they were not one family, but many families making up a whole nation. Having arrived at Sinai as a motley band of runaway slaves, they had needed a national constitution (God's law), a center of government and worship (the sanctuary), and all kinds of organization. Now everything was in place. At last the divine glory cloud lifted from its place over the sanctuary, and they set out as planned in precise military order (Num. 10:11–28).

Excitement ran high. The Israelites were not just going on a business trip or vacation—they were on their way to a new and permanent dwelling place in a bountiful land of their own that they had never seen. They had reason to believe that in a short time they would be there.

The Israelites looked forward to "a good and large land, to a land flowing with milk and honey" (Ex. 3:8). That is nothing compared to what is in store for us—a whole new earth in which we will eat from the tree of life and drink from the water of life. "Eye has not seen, nor ear heard, nor have entered into the heart of man the things which God has prepared for those who love Him" (1 Cor. 2:9). We look forward to a land of no suffering, sorrow, or regrets, and to magnificent homes designed and built by God Himself. Best of all, we will not need a sanctuary or temple to give us limited access to the Lord, because we will be able to approach Him face to face (Rev. 21; 22; see also John 14:1-3).

Chapter 5

CHALLENGES ON THE WAY
(Numbers 11; 12)

Warning for Whining

A few hours into a multiday road trip, a small voice queries, "Daddy, are we there yet?"

"No, dear, we are just getting started," comes the reply.

An hour later: "Daddy, are we nearly there?"

"No, it will take a lot longer."

A half hour later the voice whines impatiently, "Daddy, are we there yet?"

"No, dear."

A wail ensues. "I'm tired of this. I want to go home now!"

The Israelites marched for a few days, with the ark of the Lord's covenant in front of them and His cloud above them (Num. 10:33, 34). But traveling through the rough terrain of the Sinai Peninsula was a lot harder than camping on the broad plain in front of the Lord's mountain. So some started to complain, no doubt blaming Moses for their discomfort and questioning the wisdom of his leadership. Their reaction did not escape the notice of the Lord, who took it personally because He was in charge and was doing everything that He could for His people. So His fire burned in their midst and did some damage at the edge of the camp (Num. 11:1; contrast Ex. 3:2—burning in a bush that was not consumed). Therefore, Moses named the place Taberah, "place of burning" (Num. 11:3).

The Lord's fire could be friendly, as when it consumed the inaugural sacrifices on the altar (Lev. 9:24). But the Israelites well knew what His firepower could do when He was displeased. It had dramatically executed two of His priests when they failed to follow crucial instructions (Lev. 10:1, 2). So the fire blazing among the people right in their midst must have severely traumatized them.

The text does not say what the Lord's fire burned up at the outskirts of the camp. However, it is clear that this area, outside the core encampment of the 12 tribes, was where the "mixed multitude" would have had their tents. So it appears that they could have been the chief complainers.

The mixed multitude, who left Egypt with the Israelites (Ex. 12:38), were non-Israelites or of mixed descent (Lev. 24:10). Apparently God's displays of power and favor on behalf of His people had impressed them, and they had decided to cast in their lot with Israel. Their lack of "pedigree" among the chosen descendants of Jacob was not a problem for God, and He allowed them to join the Israelites in seeking to enjoy the covenant blessings. But once they made their decision to follow Him, He expected them to live under His leadership the same as the rest of the covenant community.

The mixed multitude had not suffered the rigors of slavery as the Israelites had. So they would not have been accustomed to the hardship and physical exertion they encountered on the way to Canaan. Furthermore, their worldview and religious orientation was mostly Egyptian and pagan. Egyptian culture and thinking had also affected Israel, and they had lost important aspects of their unique heritage. But they had remained separate enough to preserve a measure of their distinct identity as the Lord's people. The mixed multitude did not even have this much. So the Lord was foreign to them, and they had not yet developed loyalty to Him.

Taberah was not the first place at which the Israelite community complained. When Pharaoh's army loomed on the horizon at the Red Sea, they had cried out to the Lord (Ex.14:10) and then said to Moses:

"Is it because there were no graves in Egypt that you have taken us away to die in the wilderness? Why have you dealt with us in this way, bringing us out of Egypt? Is this not the word that we spoke to you in Egypt, saying, 'Leave us alone that we may serve the Egyptians'? For it would have been better for us to serve the Egyptians than to die in the wilderness" (verses 11, 12, NASB).

Graves in Egypt? Of course Egypt was full of graves, some of which were ancient then and are still the most prominent in the world: the pyramids. It was a land that venerated death.

The last of the Lord's 10 plagues, which struck the Egyptian firstborn, gave plenty more death to venerate and added a lot of graves (Ex. 12:29, 30).

The words "Is it because there were no graves in Egypt" were a rhetorical way to accuse Moses of being a fool for bringing them out of Egypt just to be buried. It was an accusation that Moses would later hear too many times: His leadership was bringing disaster upon the Israelites, and they would have been better off slaving away under Pharaoh. Absence made the heart grow strangely fonder. "I want to go home now!"

By blaming Moses, the Israelites ignored the fact that he was only following God's orders. So they were really implying that God was a fool. Needless to say, it was a dangerous insult.

By itself, complaining to the Lord is not necessarily a wrong thing to do. People of God such as Job, David, and Habakkuk have expressed unhappiness, distress, frustration, and even blazing anger (Job 3; Ps. 109; Hab. 1:1-2:1). Our trust in God's wisdom and love may falter, but He understands that severe stress can confuse us. If we take our troubles to Him, whatever our state of mind may be, we acknowledge His leadership in our lives, and He can then help us.

A terrible high-speed highway crash near San Francisco in 1982, caused by a young man drunk and high on drugs, almost killed my wife and me. His Chevy Nova crossed the median on Interstate 580 and crashed head-on into a Volkswagen. The collision instantly killed the driver, mangled her two daughters, and threw her car airborne onto the hood of our small Datsun B-210. Then a tractor-trailer coming behind us plowed into the steep bank by the road in order to keep from running over us. His big rig jackknifed and violently shuddered to a halt 15 feet behind our wrecked car. Stunned, Connie and I hugged each other, realizing it was a divine miracle that we had survived by fractions of seconds when physics went wild.

Aside from Connie's concussion, my cracked rib, and whiplash injuries to our backs and necks, it took a while for the full effects of our trauma to sink in. We had been working brutally hard barely to survive financially while we were full-time students. The accident exhausted our nervous and physical energies, and we could no longer keep up the pace. My goal of completing a Ph.D. to prepare for the career to which God had called me seemed hopelessly out of reach. I was confused, frustrated, angry, deeply depressed, and inclined to blame God for the situation. But my complaints were at least implicitly to God as the Lord of my life, and He brought us through. I learned to trust Him because He never let us down, even when the going got tough.

At the Red Sea the Israelites faced mortal danger, and they did cry out to God (Ex. 14:10). That was completely understandable. However, when they turned to blaming Moses, their complaining took an ugly twist, because they were denying God's leadership (verses 11, 12). Nevertheless, He overlooked the insult and delivered them in a spectacular way (verses 19-30). He was patient with them because they were "babies" in faith, and His strategy had the desired effect: "When Israel saw the great power which the Lord had used against the Egyptians, the people feared the Lord, and they believed in the Lord and in His servant Moses" (verse 31, NASB).

Unfortunately, that wasn't the end of their complaining. Between the Red Sea and Mount Sinai the Israelites grumbled against Moses (or Moses and Aaron) several more times when they lacked water and food. Each time the Lord miraculously met their need and did not discipline them (Ex. 15:22-25; 16:2-36; 17:1-7). On the last of these occasions, the Israelites had "tempted the Lord, saying, 'Is the Lord among us or not?'" (Ex. 17:7). Here was the basic question that they had implied each time they grumbled. Now it was explicit. They knew what they were doing, and the next time they would be accountable for it.

It came a year later at Taberah (Num. 11:1). The Lord did a lot for the Israelites during that year. He helped them gain victory over the Amalekites at Rephidim (Ex. 17:8-16), proclaimed His Ten Commandments from Mount Sinai (Ex. 20), issued additional laws through Moses (Ex. 21-23), established His covenant with them as a bond in blood (Ex. 24), gave plans for building the sanctuary (Ex. 25-31), and renewed the covenant with them (Ex. 33; 34) after they broke it by worshipping a golden calf (Ex. 32). When the Israelites finished the sanctuary and the Lord moved in (Ex. 35-40), He provided detailed instructions for worship and purity (Lev. 1-17) and for a holy lifestyle (Lev. 18-27). He organized the people and their camp and provided more instructions in preparation for their conquest of Canaan (Num. 1-10). Meanwhile, they were totally dependent on Him for their food through a miracle that He gave them every single day: the provision of manna (Ex. 16).

No longer were the Israelites a ragtag bunch of runaway slaves. They were now a well-constituted nation accountable to God for keeping their part of the treaty with Him that they had voluntarily contracted. He had been defending them, feeding them and providing them with water, and dwelling among them. As a result they no longer had any excuse for even implying the question: "Is the Lord among us or not?"

All this is the background to the Lord's response to their complaints at Taberah, where He first disciplined them for grumbling. If you read about this episode in isolation from its context, you could get the impression that the Lord was harshly overreacting. In reality He was mercifully giving them a "warning ticket" that they should not soon forget.

Ironically, it was only when the Israelites pleaded with Moses for help and he prayed to the Lord for them that the divine fire subsided (Num. 11:2). Usually their grumbling was directed against Moses. As did Job's friends (Job 42:7-9), they discovered that they were dependent on the one they had wronged to intercede for them. They had to humbly confess to Moses that they were at fault before God would accept their repentance.

If we wrong people, we cannot bypass reconciliation with them by just going straight to God. Jesus said: "Therefore if you bring your gift to the altar, and there remember that your brother has something against you, leave your gift there before the altar, and go your way. First be reconciled to your brother, and then come and offer your gift" (Matt. 5:23, 24). It was not a new concept. According to God's instructions, Israelites who defrauded another person through a false oath were responsible for restoring what they had wrongfully taken or kept, plus 20 percent (Lev. 6:1-5). Making such reparation naturally required confession to the wronged individual (cf. Lev. 5:5). Only after putting things right with that person was the sinner allowed to offer a sacrifice to the Lord and receive forgiveness (Lev. 6:6, 7).

Zacchaeus realized that obtaining forgiveness from God does not mean declaring bankruptcy on our obligations to other people. He promised: "Look, Lord, I give half of my goods to the poor; and if I have taken anything from anyone by false accusation, I restore fourfold" (Luke 19:8). Jesus accepted his promise, replying: "Today salvation has come to this house, because he also is a son of Abraham; for the Son of Man has come to seek and to save that which was lost" (verses 9, 10).

Indeed, confession is good for the soul! God taught the Israelites that at Taberah, where they escaped divine fire. He also gives the rest of the human race an opportunity to learn it before His fire moves into our neighborhood—Planet Earth—and consumes those who reject the intercession of His only-begotten Son (Heb. 4:14-16; 7:25; 1 John 1:9; Rev. 14:9-12; 19:20; 20:9-15; 21:8).

Lust of the Fleshpots

Alas, the fiery warning at Taberah was not enough for the Israelites. When things cooled down, they were at it again. "The riffraff in their midst felt a gluttonous craving; and then the Israelites wept and said, 'If only we had meat to eat! We remember the fish that we used to eat free in Egypt, the cucumbers, the melons, the leeks, the onions, and the garlic. Now our gullets are shriveled. There is nothing at all! Nothing but this manna to look to!'" (Num. 11:4-6, Tanakh).

55

The "riffraff" were the "mixed multitude" (cf. Ex. 12:38). The Bible only implies their role at Taberah (see above), but here it is plain. These mixed-up people incited a mutiny of gluttony. It was not that they were going hungry. They already had an abundance of delicious, nutritious food perfectly designed for their health by the divine dietitian (see Exodus 16:31 and Numbers 11:8 regarding the taste). He promised that if they cooperated with all His prescriptions, they would suffer none of the diseases that afflicted the Egyptians (Ex. 15:26). Neither was there anything wrong with the service: God Himself was the caterer, and He was always on time.

The riffraff grumbled when their tummies rumbled for "Mom's home cookin' down in good ole Egypt." Ah yes, there were fish, and healthy vegetables and melons. But they were side dishes or for flavoring. The main course was meat. Forget about the heavenly granola out here in the desert. Give us McDonald's, Kentucky Fried Chicken, and our home barbecue! We're not getting our minimum daily requirement of cholesterol and carcinogens! Needless to say, turning their noses up at God's manna was a huge insult to Him.

The Israelites had had a tougher life in Egypt than the riffraff, so they didn't remember as much luxury. But pretty soon the discontent spread to them, and whining grew to weeping, as if they were starving.

The people didn't need any commercials to whip up their craving by telling them that it was all about gratifying taste, rather than satisfying their needs with what was good for them.

This approach to diet is gluttony. Gluttony is not only overeating in general, but also disregarding health in favor of taste, which can easily become perverted. As a result, gluttony is one of the cardinal sins of some affluent modern societies, such as that of the United States. The cost in suffering, work loss, and medical treatment is stupendous.

Also problematic is cherishing a craving for something that may be nutritionally good, but is not available to you unless you disregard the Lord's leading. God made "the tree of the knowledge of good and evil" in the garden of Eden, and Eve was undoubtedly accurate in her visual assessment that it was good for food (Gen. 3:6). But that didn't make it right for her to eat it, because God had declared it off-limits (Gen. 2:17). The riffraff and Israelites craved some healthy items: cucumbers, melons, leeks, onions, and garlic. But those were back in Egypt and did not grow in the wilderness through which the Lord was leading them. Longing for them meant desiring Egypt, which involved not wanting to go to the Promised Land with the Lord.

Understandably, the Lord was angry. Moses was upset too (Num. 11:10). Now the Israelites were in mortal danger. After the golden calf incident, Moses had interceded for them by saying to God, "Yet now, if You will forgive their sin—but if not, I pray, blot me out of Your book which You have written" (Ex. 32:32). At Taberah he had prayed in order to intervene for them again (Num. 11:2). Now he talked to the Lord, all right, but his interest in intercession had died a natural death. They were being completely unreasonable, and their failure to learn was intolerable, even for a most patient man. Moses blamed the Lord for laying the burden of all these childish people on him. To get out of his miserable situation, he wanted to die an unnatural death (verses 11-15).

Moses has not been the only discouraged pastor in history. Elijah, who fled from the royal witch Jezebel, found himself sitting under a broom tree, and prayed that he might die (1 Kings 19:4). Isaiah was distressed by the moral state of his nation, which was full of "wounds and bruises and putrefying sores" (Isa. 1:6).

The Lord cares about His discouraged ministers and is remarkably gentle with them. He knows from experience what they feel like when people give them a hard time. Rather than rebuking them, He sensitively gives them what they need to encourage them and get them going again. After the stress of the golden calf episode, He provided Moses a glimpse of His glory (Ex. 33:18-34:8). After Elijah's exhausting escape from the ruthless queen, an angel twice brought him food and water (1 Kings 19:5-8), and the Lord revealed Himself and His plan for the prophet in a still small voice (verses 12-18). When Isaiah was young and his motivation for ministry had almost perished in the face of apparently insurmountable obstacles, God jump-started his spiritual battery with an awesome vision of divine glory in the Temple (Isa. 6).

The Lord has concern for His modern pastors, too. Bill Allison became a youth pastor at the age of 22 and got off to a rough start. He tells what happened:

"During the very first week I served in that church as youth pastor, each of the people who voted against my coming to the church decided to drop in and visit me. They came into my office one at a time and said the most hurtful things—doing their absolute best to discourage me. (Have you ever noticed that some people in church seem to believe that discouragement and criticism are their spiritual gifts—and that they want to use them on you?) 'Students will never like you,' one snorted as I imagined little horns starting to protrude from his head. Another told me in no uncertain terms that I was 'out of the will of God' for accepting the position—and was so angry that she got her tail caught in the door of my office as she stormed out. Another held her pitchfork tightly and flatly said, 'You will ruin this church.' With the exception of the horns, tail, and pitchfork—everything in this story is as it happened."

Rather than giving up, Allison specifically asked the Lord to provide what he needed to continue in His work. God has met those needs ever since.[1]

In response to the bitter complaint of Moses when the Israelites groused about their manna and demanded meat (Num. 11:1-16), the Lord provided two practical solutions, both of which required His miraculous intervention. First, He put His Spirit on 70 chosen elders, individuals already regarded by their people as leaders. They would help Moses bear the burden of managing the community (verses 16, 17, 24-30). That way Moses could delegate responsibility, facilitate communication to the various segments of the Israelite nation through their representatives, and allow the large and powerful committee to share blame when the Israelites came up with any grievances against their leadership. No longer would Moses be the sole lightning rod for all criticism.

When the Spirit came upon the elders, they prophesied on that occasion, but not after that (verse 25-30). The Bible does not record what they said. The fact that they prophesied, rather than what they said, was the main point. It showed that God had accepted them in their new role of assisting Moses.

Associate leaders appointed by God and validated by the Holy Spirit are also good for the modern Christian church (compare Jesus' 70 disciples, Luke 10). It is unhealthy to place too much burden on any one individual. Those who are chosen should already be credible leaders among the groups they represent. Never should they be unrecognized individuals artificially imposed upon those segments.

God's second practical solution was to give the Israelites what they asked for: meat, and lots of it. When He told Moses that He planned to provide them more meat than they could eat every day for a whole month, Moses was incredulous. The logistics of providing that much for 600,000 men, plus women and children, were beyond his comprehension (Num. 11:18-22). Yet he was the same Moses who had stood on the shore of the Red Sea and announced: "Do not be afraid. Stand still, and see the salvation of the Lord, which He will accomplish for you today. For the Egyptians whom you see today, you shall see again no more forever" (Ex. 14:13). Moses had been involved in astounding miracles, so He should have known by now that nothing was impossible for God when there was a real need. But why would the Lord perform a miracle of such magnitude just to answer a trivial complaint?

The miracle was not merely about food. The Lord could not lead His people to victory in the Promised Land while they were still longing for life in Egypt under rule opposed to Him. An army that grouses about its rations will quail before a powerful enemy. If the Israelites couldn't live without meat now, they would soon become dead meat. So He needed to teach them a lesson of biblical proportions by giving them what they wanted in such a way that they would realize how stupid they were. He had Moses announce that they would have meat for a month "until it comes out of your nostrils and becomes loathsome to you, because you have despised the Lord who is among you, and have wept before Him, saying, 'Why did we ever come up out of Egypt?'" (Num. 11:20).

The Lord's strategy was like that of a father whose young son wanted to try smoking.

The father decided to cure his tobacco curiosity once and for all, no ifs, ands, or butts about it. So he lit a cigarette, put it in the lad's mouth, and told him to breathe in hard. The boy quickly wanted to quit, but his dad made him smoke the whole cigarette until his eyes and nose were streaming, and he was gasping for air and violently coughing. The experience was so miserable that he was never even tempted to smoke again.

Meat came in the form of quail, which arrived in huge numbers and flew low enough above the surface of the ground (to about three feet) all around the camp of the Israelites, so that they could easily catch the helpless birds. The people were so greedy that they slaughtered them all day, all night, and all the next day. They each gathered at least 10 homers (Num. 11:32). Given that a homer (originally "donkey load") was about six bushels, each of them collected more than 60 bushels. If only the 600,000 men (verse 21) had 60 bushels each (perhaps with the women and children helping them), the total was more than 36 million bushels. And if each bushel contained only five birds each, the Israelites killed more than 180 million birds! There must have been dead birds around the camp as far as the eye could see.

It is true that many quail naturally migrate over the Sinai Peninsula, which forms a land bridge between Africa and Asia. With their heavy bodies, they rely on winds to assist their long flights, which exhaust them. In the 1900s Arabs of that region are known to have caught 1 to 2 million of them with nets. But only a wind from the Lord (verse 31) could bring the number of quail reported in Numbers 11.

Then the Israelites (with the riffraff) sat down and started to gorge themselves. They had enough quail to eat for a month (cf. verse 20), but the Lord did not waste time letting them enjoy it. He had tested their loyalty to Him by giving them what they wanted, and they had miserably flunked, just as Adam and Eve failed their test of loyalty (Gen. 3).

God warned Adam and Eve that eating forbidden food would result in their death (Gen. 2:17). However, although they became mortal on the day they transgressed, He mercifully allowed them to continue living for a while. They sinned, but because they did not fully comprehend the implications of what they did, there was hope for them to repent. Unlike Adam and Eve, the Israelites had received plenty of opportunities to know exactly what they were doing. Many of them already showed that they were beyond redemption. So the Lord purged them out of the community. On the day they ate of the quail, they surely died.

"But while the meat was still between their teeth, before it was consumed, the anger of the Lord was kindled against the people, and the Lord struck the people with a very great plague. So that place was called Kibroth-hattaavah, because there they buried the people who had the craving" (Num. 11:33, 34, NRSV).

The text does not describe the nature of the plague or how many people it killed, but apparently the body count was high. The name of the place means "the graves of craving."

With slick advertising pioneered by the serpent in Eden, the world tells us that desire justifies all. John, the beloved disciple of Christ, disagreed:

"Do not love the world or the things in the world. If anyone loves the world, the love of the Father is not in him. For all that is in the world—the lust of the flesh, the lust of the eyes, and the pride of life—is not of the Father but is of the world. And the world is passing away, and the lust of it; but he who does the will of God abides forever" (1 John 2:15-17).

Jesus showed us the way. Even after He had fasted for 40 days and was desperately weak from hunger, He refused to be disloyal to His Father by turning even one stone into bread (Matt. 4:1-4). Performing such a miracle was not difficult by itself—later Jesus did something similar when He provided loaves and fish for a multitude (Matt. 14). The problem was the source of the suggestion—the devil, who was expressing doubt that Jesus was the Son of God and asking Him to prove it. So He replied, "It is written, 'Man shall not live by bread alone, but by every word that proceeds from the mouth of God' " (Matt. 4:4). Those who live by the Word of the Lord, the source of life, will not end up in graves of craving.

Power and Racism

Harsh criticism is hard to take, but it is especially rough when it comes from close family members. They are the people whom you love and trust, who have a vested interest in you. Because they have been with you for a long time, perhaps even from the time you were born, they know you inside and out.

When the Israelites complained about food, they were indirectly attacking the leadership of God and Moses, who had brought them from Egypt (Num. 11:4-6, 18, 20). That greatly upset Moses, who wished that he might die and poured out a bitter speech to the Lord (verses 11-15).

Now poor Moses faced something worse: direct criticism of his leadership from Miriam and Aaron, his own sister and brother. "Miriam and Aaron spoke against Moses because of the Cushite woman he had married: 'He married a Cushite woman!' They said, 'Has the Lord spoken only through Moses? Has He not spoken through us as well?'" (Num. 12:1, 2, Tanakh).

Their attitude so stunned Moses that he was speechless. He was a very humble man (verse 3), which is why God was able to use him without his ego getting in the way. Can you imagine what the church and world would be like if everyone were like him, so that egos didn't block peace, cooperation, and progress? Moses would powerfully defend the Lord's honor, even with righteous rage (Ex. 32:19-30, for example), but was not at all inclined to stick up for himself, even to his siblings.

It was big sister Miriam who had watched over Moses when he floated as a baby among the reeds by the Nile River (Ex. 2:4, 7, 8). "Miriam the prophetess" led the women of Israel in rejoicing after the deliverance at the Red Sea (Ex. 15:20, 21). Aaron had been Moses' spokesman to the Israelites and Pharaoh in Egypt (Ex. 4:14-16, 29, 30; 5:1) and was the one whom Moses had anointed as high priest (Lev. 8:12). Centuries later the Lord affirmed the crucial role of Miriam and Aaron as the partners of Moses in leading the Israelites: "For I brought you up from the land of Egypt, I redeemed you from the house of bondage; and I sent before you Moses, Aaron, and Miriam" (Micah 6:4).

What went wrong? The fact that Numbers 12:1 mentions Miriam before Aaron suggests that she instigated the criticism of Moses for having married "a Cushite woman." It is true that Moses had married a non-Israelite woman because of his circumstances after fleeing from Egypt (Ex. 3). But Zipporah was Midianite, and we find no evidence elsewhere that she was even partly Cushite. Nor does the Bible say that Zipporah had died, or indicate that Moses married a second wife while she was living.

It appears that Miriam, followed by Aaron, referred to Zipporah as an Ethiopian or Sudanese. This would have been a racial slur to exaggerate the darker color of Zipporah's skin, regard her as inferior on that basis, and therefore lower Moses a notch or two. It appears that jealousy motivated the sister. Zipporah had never endured oppression in Egypt, and it was only after the Israelites were safely in the wilderness that she rejoined Moses (Ex. 18:1-6). Now she would have been regarded as the "first lady" of Israel, displacing Miriam.

But why would Miriam and Aaron want to reduce Moses to their level? The main issue in this sibling rivalry was power—the power of leadership through the prophetic gift. "They said, 'Has the Lord spoken only through Moses? Has He not spoken through us also?'" (Num. 12:2). Why would this come up now? According to the previous chapter (Num. 11), Moses had appointed 70 elders to help him govern the people. The Lord had taken some of the Spirit that was on Moses and put it on them, so that they shared his prophetic gift (verses 16, 17, 24-30). This was God's idea, not his. However, Miriam and Aaron would have felt displaced by the 70 elders, whom Moses had appointed without consulting them.

The Lord heard what Miriam and Aaron were saying, which indirectly criticized Him (Num. 12:2). He summoned them to come with Moses to His sanctuary headquarters so that He could arbitrate their domestic dispute (verses 4, 5). God did not deny that He had given Miriam and Aaron the gift of prophecy (verse 6). But He reminded them that He had assigned Moses a special role. Their brother was more than a prophet: "He is faithful in all My house. I speak with him face to face, even plainly, and not in dark sayings; and he sees the form of the Lord" (verses 7, 8). Moses was unique then and later. After he died, the biblical writer declared that "there has not arisen in Israel a prophet like Moses, whom the Lord knew face to face" (Deut. 34:10).

Miriam and Aaron already knew that the Lord had chosen to use Moses in a special way. So the Lord's logical question to them was: "Why then were you not afraid to speak against My servant Moses?" (Num. 12:8). As the Lord departed in anger, Miriam found herself stricken with a scaly skin disease that made her skin appear like snow (verses 9, 10; for similar divine punishment, see also 2 Kings 5:27; 15:5; 2 Chronicles 26:20).

"Like snow" could refer to flaky texture, but it would likely also describe skin as bright white. Miriam's punishment fitted her crime. She had belittled Moses' wife for her skin. Now Miriam's own skin was a mess. In fact, it was probably much lighter in color than normal, as if God were saying: "You don't think dark is beautiful? OK, see how you like the opposite!"

That is what God thinks of racism. It is moral leprosy. Unfortunately, racism is still with us in modern times. The 2004 film *Hotel Rwanda* tells the true story of Paul Rusesabagina and his efforts to save more than 1,000 people from the Rwandan genocide of 1994. Racism was the root of that country's strife, which led to the deaths of more than 800,000 people.

Like Moses and Zipporah, Paul and his wife, Tatiana, were of different ethnic groups. Paul was Hutu, and Tatiana was Tutsi. Belgian colonists had stressed the differences between the two tribes about 1900 when they called those with longer noses and lighter skin (more European-looking) "Tutsis" and appointed them to leadership roles over all the rest, whom they dubbed "Hutus." From this favoritism and resulting antagonism arose a power struggle. Paul Rusesabagina, at first only wishing to shield his Tutsi wife and their children, ended up sheltering more than 1,000 Tutsis and moderate Hutus in the hotel that he managed.[2]

Racism, like sin itself, is universal. Existing in every land and every age, it not only prompts brutal ethnic cleansing, but spreads more subtly into workplaces, schools, and churches. Not only is it unfair because people are born with their race and cannot change it

(Jer. 13:23)—it is an insult to God, who created all His human children from one common ancestry (Acts 17:26). It is about power, giving excuses to marginalize, exploit, oppress, or blame those who are not just like us in order to build ourselves up or protect ourselves at their expense.

Rosa Parks and Martin Luther King, Jr., are resting in peace. However, their work is not yet finished, even in the Christian church. It is easy and comfortable to be in a state of denial, dismissing racism as long ago or far away. But, starting with our own hearts, we need to root out the quiet but deadly prejudices, discriminations, apartheids, and slaveries that linger among us. Rather than advocating mere "tolerance," we should revel in the richness of our God-given diversity, drawing on all our different strengths within the dynamic, unified body of Christ (cf. 1 Cor. 12).

Unity in our multicultural global community, which can dramatically testify to the power of Christ among us, takes time, thought, sensitivity, and lots of honest, open communication. Through cooperation with God we accept His gift of love through the Holy Spirit (Rom. 5:5). And it opens to us the intercession of Jesus, who prayed on behalf of all His followers shortly before He was betrayed for being the different kind of person He was: "That they all may be one, as You, Father, are in Me, and I in You; that they also may be one in Us, that the world may believe that You sent Me. And the glory which You gave Me I have given them, that they may be one just as We are one: I in them, and You in Me; that they may be made perfect in one, and that the world may know that You have sent Me, and have loved them as You have loved Me" (John 17:21-23).

Redemption exists even for the sin of racism. Aaron, the high priest, was the appointed intercessor for his people. But he begged for forgiveness on behalf of himself and Miriam, and for the healing of his sister, whose decomposing appearance reflected the deadly attitude that she had expressed toward Zipporah and Moses (Num. 12:11, 12). As at Taberah, Moses interceded (verse 13; cf. Num. 11:2). Miriam was healed. However, because she was a leader, her sin and restoration was a public matter. Having attempted to exclude

Zipporah in order to damage the leadership of Moses, the Lord's servant, she was now banished from the camp for seven days before the Israelites traveled on. Years before Miriam had waited for Moses at the Nile River. This time he and the whole community waited for her (Num. 12:14, 15).

[1] http://timschmoyer.com/2008/01/15/leading-when-you-want-to-quit-1-of-4.
[2] http://news.nationalgeographic.com/news/2004/12/1209_041209_hotel_rwanda.html; http://en.wikipedia.org/wiki/Tutsi.

Chapter 6

SNATCHING DEFEAT FROM THE JAWS OF VICTORY
(Numbers 13-15)

Military "Intelligence"

Having entered the Wilderness of Paran (Num. 12:16), the Israelites now neared Canaan. It was time to begin preparations for the invasion! The Lord already knew everything about the land, but He wanted to involve the people in the planning process so that they would know what to expect and not be surprised in a way that would terrify them. They needed to understand the strength of the enemy and decide on victory with the Lord before going into battle, when second thoughts would be disastrous. Also they could benefit from an encouraging report on the superior quality of the land. According to the Lord, it was "flowing with milk and honey" (Ex. 3:8, 17; 13:5), but none of them had ever seen it.

The big question was: Did the Israelites have enough faith in God to allow Him to lead them through difficult obstacles? Already He had miraculously brought them safely out of Egypt, through the Red Sea, and across the wilderness. But they had repeatedly questioned whether He was really with them. Would they do that again?

God was eager to deliver the Promised Land to loyal people, who would serve as His channel of revelation to the world. In the relative privacy of the wilderness He had trained, organized, and disciplined them for this moment. But the training was over. This was the real thing.

Once the Israelites stepped into their own land, they would be on the world stage. The way they acted there would powerfully reflect on the character of God. He could not allow disloyal Israelites to possess Canaan. If He did that, He would destroy any hope of properly representing His character of love (including justice and mercy) to the other inhabitants of Planet Earth so that they would turn to Him and be saved.

As the Aaronic priests were to the Israelites, so the Israelites were to other nations: "a kingdom of priests" (Ex. 19:6). Just as the Lord did not tolerate misrepresentation of Himself by His Aaronic priests, which would convey the wrong message to His people (Lev. 10—Nadab and Abihu), neither would He allow His people to depict Him falsely before the rest of the world. He could not bless them unless all families of the earth could be blessed through them (Gen. 12:3; 22:18).

In order to give the Israelites the opportunity to make an informed and firm decision to take the land, the Lord instructed Moses to send in scouts, who would bring back a detailed report regarding various aspects of it. The men were to be leaders representing every tribe, individuals whose opinions would be credible to the various sectors of the Israelite community (Num. 13:1-20). Since the way to the hearts of the people was through their stomachs, it was a strategic time for the mission of the scouts: "the season of the first ripe grapes" (verse 20).

According to Deuteronomy 1:22, 23, the people themselves came up with the idea to send in scouts, and Moses liked the suggestion. When we put this information with Numbers 13, we can conclude that apparently the Lord then approved the plan and told Moses to go ahead with it. Divine leading does not rule out human initiative, as long as people cooperate with God. Earlier, when the Israelites set out from Sinai with the Lord guiding them, Moses had asked his Midianite relative to come along because he knew the territory and could give practical advice (Num. 10:29-34).

The scouts did not just take a little peek. They spent 40 days covering an extensive itinerary. Then they returned to the Israelite camp at Kadesh, in the Wilderness of Paran, for "show and tell." They brought back samples: some pomegranates, figs, and a single cluster of grapes so gigantic they had to carry it between two of them on a pole (Num. 13:21-26). The people must have been astounded. Forget the fleshpots, onions, and garlic of Egypt! Home would be sweet indeed. By its fruits they knew it.

The scouts affirmed the Lord's assessment of Canaan as "flowing with milk and honey." But most of them stressed the military strength of the nations there and the fact that their populations filled the land (verses 27-29). The implication was that it would be fool-hardy to attempt an invasion.

The scout from the tribe Judah had a minority opinion: "Caleb hushed the people before Moses and said, 'Let us by all means go up, and we shall gain possession of it, for we shall surely overcome it'" (verse 30, Tanakh). For Caleb, his "we" included God. He was sec-onding the motion of Moses, who had encouraged the Israelites before the scouts' mission: "Look, the Lord your God has set the land before you; go up and possess it, as the Lord God of your fathers has spoken to you; do not fear or be discouraged" (Deut. 1:21).

The other scouts retorted with a blanket contradiction: "We are not able to go up against the people, for they are stronger than we" (Num. 13:31). For them, "we" excluded God. To win the vote of the people, who liked the fruit they saw, the scouts exaggerated the negative. They claimed that the land was dangerous for everyone who lived in it, that all the people they saw were huge, and that they were like grasshoppers before the giants there (verses 32, 33).

The faithless attitude of the spies provoked a meltdown of un-precedented complaint, grief, and open rebellion. Forget about God and Moses. "Let us select a leader and return to Egypt" (Num. 14:4). Stuck in a mental rut, they were still slaves at heart. Looking at only their own strength would lead them straight back to bondage.

Centuries later in a German cloister the young monk Martin Luther was also a slave at heart. By fasting, vigils, and whippings, he desperately but vainly tried to earn spiritual deliverance. But then he found the way to freedom and peaceful assurance by accepting God's ability in place of his own. If only the Israelites could have had an experience like that!

Two scouts made a passionate appeal, which turned out to be the final "altar call." They were Joshua of the tribe of Ephraim, who was the assistant of Moses and the military leader of Israel who had led in the defeat of Amalek (cf. Ex. 17:9, 10, 13; 24:13; 33:11; Num. 11:28), and Caleb. Tearing their clothes to express their anguish, they extolled the glory of the Promised Land, urged the people not to rebel against the Lord, and insisted that because He was with them, they had nothing to fear from the God-forsaken Canaanites (Num. 14:6-9). Faithful Caleb and Joshua received nothing for their trouble but the unanimous outcry to stone them (verse 10).

That was it. Enough. Period. The glory of the Lord appeared and intervened. It stopped the stoning, but by condemning the Lord's true servants to death, the apostate adult community passed on themselves an irrevocable sentence (cf. Acts 7:54-60, in which Stephen was actually stoned). The Lord could never use them as His channel of revelation. So they could never enter Canaan.

As He had after the golden calf fiasco (Ex. 32:10), the Lord told Moses that He would destroy them and make of Moses a great nation (Num. 14:10-12). Again Moses interceded. He appealed to God's need to preserve His reputation among the nations (verses 13-16; cf. Ex. 32:11, 12) and to His character of mercy (Num. 14:17-19), which He had proclaimed to Moses (Ex. 34:6, 7).

The Lord did forgive Israel on the corporate level (Num. 14:20), which meant that He would allow the nation to continue for the sake of His reputation. However, also for the sake of maintaining His glory in the world, the entire adult generation that He had brought out of Egypt, except for faithful Caleb and Joshua, would die in the wilderness. Only their children below the age of 20 would enter the Promised Land when they had grown up (verses 21-35). To make the punishment fit the crime, the Israelites would wander in the wilderness 40 years, a year for each day of the scouts' journey (verse 34). As the "firstfruits" of death, to show that the Lord meant what He said, the 10 unfaithful spies who had triggered the rebellion immediately died from a plague (verses 36-38).

When Moses reported the Lord's sentence upon the Israelites and announced that they were heading back into the desert (verses 25, 39), they did not want to accept the turn of events. Rather, they claimed that they were now ready to obey God's former instruction to take the land. So they tried to storm Canaan on their own, without divine approval or aid. Of course they miserably failed (verses 40-45). They had refused to cooperate with the Lord in any way. When He said "Go!" they halted, and when He said "Stop!" they rushed ahead. His former command was no longer in effect. They had lost their opportunity.

Our Delay in Entering the Heavenly "Promised Land"

If we take some time to pause from our hectic schedules and crammed agendas to reflect on the biblical story, its implications for us are sobering. If we belong to Christ, we are spiritual descendants of Abraham, and "heirs according to the promise" (Gal. 3:29). Heirs of what? The Lord promised to Abraham that his descendants would become a great nation, have their own land, and be a blessing to all peoples (Gen. 12:1-3; 22:17, 18).

Now the invitation to receive salvation goes directly to Gentiles who believe in Christ, so their connection to Abraham is spiritual rather than requiring them to join an ethnic nation (Acts 15). Abraham's "great nation" is vaster than he ever imagined, incorporating people from all parts of the earth. Their mission is to bring blessing to all the inhabitants of the planet by sharing with them the source of blessing: the one descendant of Abraham—Jesus Christ (Gal. 3:16).

So what land do the Lord's spiritual Israelites inherit? His people of faith "desire a better, that is, a heavenly country. Therefore God is not ashamed to be called their God, for He has prepared a city for them" (Heb. 11:16). The last two chapters of the Bible describe this heavenly city, which comes down to a glorious new earth that God prepares for His people (Rev. 21; 22). It is our final home, our Promised Land, many times bigger and better than the ancient country promised to the Israelites.

Canaan flowed with milk and honey, but the new earth flows with the water of life, and there is no flow of tears there. Canaan had huge grape clusters, but the new earth has the tree of life. Canaan had cities, but the new earth has the New Jerusalem. Canaan had

71

sunshine, but the new earth has the glory of God.

The Lord has already promised our home to us (see also John 14:1-3), just as He promised Canaan to the Israelites. So the new earth already belongs to us, just as Canaan did to them. We must only follow His leading in order to go up and possess it, just as the Israelites only had to follow God in order to have Canaan. He has provided all that we need—a new covenant, instructions, promise of victory, organization, and prophetic guidance, just as He offered everything necessary for the Israelites.

So why aren't we already home in our Promised Land? Perhaps the parallels continue. Gulp! Have generations of us died while "wandering in the wilderness" of this world? Do we share some problems with the Israelites, such as focus on obstacles, inadequate faith in the presence and leading of God among us, and insistence on material comfort and sensual gratification? It is easy to pin such faults on others, but what about our own hearts and lives?

What is the Lord waiting for? What should happen before we can go home? The Israelites were supposed to follow God's lead in carrying out an invasion. So are we. For them the invasion was military—waging war. For us it is spiritual—waging love. Jesus has given us our marching orders.

"'Go therefore and make disciples of all the nations, baptizing them in the name of the Father and of the Son and of the Holy Spirit, teaching them to observe all things that I have commanded you; and lo, I am with you always, even to the end of the age.' Amen" (Matt. 28:19, 20). "And this gospel of the kingdom will be preached in all the world as a witness to all the nations, and then the end will come" (Matt. 24:14).

When Jesus said, "and then the end will come," He meant: at that time "I will come again and receive you to Myself; that where I am, there you may be also" (John 14:3). In other words, when all nations have the opportunity to hear the gospel, Christ will come a second time and take us home. That is what God is waiting for. God does not expect that everyone will be converted. He respects the human free choice that He created and enters only the heart that is willing to receive Him (Rev. 3:20). But He is "not wishing for any to perish but for all to come to repentance" (2 Peter 3:9, NASB). So He wants to give everyone a fair chance to make an informed decision through the witness of the gospel, which testifies to His love (John 3:16; 1 John 4:8). Whether the inhabitants of earth tune in and listen or not is their business (cf. Eze. 2:5, 7), but the message should reach them.

Anyone who doubts that the Lord is serious about making sure that people have adequate opportunity to respond should remember that He gave the pre-Flood world 120 years (Gen. 6:3). In fact, He allowed the inhabitants of Canaan 400 years while His chosen people had to wait in Egypt (Gen. 15:13-16). But when God can do nothing more for people (Isa. 5:4) and they have settled into their decisions (Rev. 22:11), He comes quickly with His reward (verse 12).

There is nothing mysterious here. The Lord has plainly revealed His agenda, which is based on His character of fairness and mercy (Ex. 34:6, 7).

If it is so clear, what has been the holdup? Just think about the logistics! How are we supposed to reach all peoples of earth with the gospel? Do you have any idea how fast the world's population is growing? Did you know that a number of countries have severe laws against proselytizing, so that converting to another religion is difficult and even dangerous? What about language and cultural barriers, lack of sufficient budget and resources, the pervasive materialism and postmodernism that have destroyed interest in the God of the Bible, and the tremendous growth of temptations through avenues such as the Internet? In many ways the task confronting us is looking progressively harder, just as the Israelites' delay made conquest of Canaan more difficult because their enemies grew stronger.

What is the solution? To possess Canaan, the Israelites needed more miracles. Similarly, we need miracles to take the gospel to the whole world. Indeed, miracles are already happening, which encourages us to believe that God can do the great things that He has promised. Our formula for success is the same as it was for the Israelites and for the early disciples of Christ. Unite in trusting God, receive His power, and move forward under His leading, wholeheartedly following the Lord as Caleb did (Num. 14:24). Jesus' followers came together in prayer, obtained the power of the Holy Spirit (Acts 1; 2), and then went out and preached the gospel "to every creature under heaven" (Col. 1:23).

In Old Testament times the Lord's Spirit gave His people courage and strength for battle (Judges 3:10; 6:34; 11:29; 14:19; 15:14). It was also the Spirit who endowed His New Testament believers with the power of love for the spiritual warfare of waging love against the forces of selfishness: "Now hope does not disappoint, because the love of God has been poured out in our hearts by the Holy Spirit who was given to us" (Rom. 5:5). Love is the character of God (1 John 4:8) and therefore the basis of His law (Matt. 22:37-40). Through His Spirit, as a gift of grace received through faith, God brings us into harmony with Himself and His kind of love.

God's kind of unselfish love is the most powerful and enduring motivational force in the universe (1 Cor. 13:7, 8). "For God so loved the world that He gave His only begotten Son, that whoever believes in Him should not perish but have everlasting life" (John 3:16). This is the most amazing thing that ever happened, and it was motivated by His love.

The Lord's gift of love to us through the Spirit empowers us to do works of faith (Gal. 5:6) and to reconcile and unite with each other. Genuine, deep, and lasting unity is miraculous and holy, and it displays to the world what Christ's gospel can accomplish (Ps. 133; Mal. 4:5, 6; John 17:20-23; Acts 1; 2). Divine love compels us to participate together in God's redemptive mission by stepping out of our comfortable little boxes and ignoring obstacles, irritations, ridicule, and persecution because we are passionately eager for others to enjoy salvation through Christ.

Strong motivation through love does not mean that our gospel appeals should be insensitive, abrasive, and obnoxious, such as those employed by aggressive salespersons, including many vendors of religion. "Love suffers long and is kind; love does not envy; love does not parade itself, is not puffed up; does not behave rudely, does not seek its own, is not provoked, thinks no evil" (1 Cor. 13:4, 5).

God has put the Promised Land within our reach. For the sake of everyone, including ourselves, we can take as our motto the immortal declaration of Caleb: "Let us by all means go up, and we shall gain possession of it, for we shall surely overcome it" (Num. 13:30, Tanakh).

Serving Time or a Time of Serving?

Waiting a long time for someone else is hard, even under ideal conditions. It is even more difficult if they keep you waiting because of a stupid mistake.

Forty years is a long time. Living conditions in a wilderness are far from ideal. Rebelling against God is the ultimate stupid mistake. But it was the kind of delay that Caleb and Joshua had to endure. Their situation was much better than that of anyone else among their generation, because they alone would live to enter the Promised Land. But for four long, dreary decades they would do time out with the Israelites as the people wandered from place to place on a road to nowhere, making no progress except for the trail of graves they left behind them.

During those 40 years Caleb and Joshua should have been in Canaan along with Moses, Aaron, and Miriam, who belonged to an older generation and had already waited for decades before the Israelites left Egypt (Ex. 2:15-25; 7:7). Caleb and Joshua had planned to spend a short time evicting the former tenants of Canaan and making homes for themselves and their families. Then they could peacefully settle down under their vines and fig trees. But here they were, winners strapped to a team of certified losers. Their situation was way more than enough to induce a case of chronic depression.

It could have been a temptation for Caleb and Joshua, the master guides, to find some strong teenagers belonging to the next generation, form a Pathfinder troop, and set out to take some of Canaan for themselves. They could have felt that coming out of an Israel in that condition would be equivalent to leaving Egypt—or Babylon. But they stayed with their faulty nation and its funeral procession.

During those 40 years Caleb and Joshua did not remain idle. They had another generation to train, and their work was successful. The younger people were not perfect, but when it came time to take Canaan, they were ready, willing, and able to follow God (see the book of Joshua). More than military training, it was faith-attitude forming, theological education for new life to arise from a nation of death—a seminary from a cemetery.

Martin Luther also knew what it was like to wait in apparent isolation from his main life's work. In 1521, four years after posting his famous 95 theses on the door at Wittenberg, and just after delivering his famous speech concerning his writings at the Diet of Worms, Luther was "kidnapped." A great supporter of his, Frederick of Saxony, arranged for a company of masked horsemen to take Luther to the remote Wartburg Castle at Eisenach for his own safety.

Although Luther lived like a prisoner for nearly a year, he used it as a time of service, not just serving time. Along with other writings, he most famously translated the New Testament into German during his experience of "desert," or "Patmos," as he would later call it. It was one of his greatest and most enduring contributions to the cause of the gospel.

If we find ourselves "waiting in the wilderness," there are plenty of positive things that we can do to prepare for our entrance into the heavenly "Canaan." There are families and churches to unite, children and adults to teach, encouragements to give, neighbors to reach, and intercessory prayers to offer. Above all, we can foster faith and openness to the gift of love through the Holy Spirit. As long as we are open to God, saying yes to Him and wholeheartedly following Him all the way, we are bound for the Promised Land!

There Is Still a Future

At first glance Numbers 15:1-16 looks out of place, as if it belongs back in the book of Leviticus. Here we find instructions for grain and wine offerings to accompany all burnt offerings (cf. Lev. 1) and "sacrifices," that is, the kinds of sacrifices from which the offerer could eat (cf. Lev. 3; 7). These accompaniments to animal sacrifices completed token "meals" for God, just as Abraham had offered a full meal, including cakes of grain and drink along with meat, to the Lord and His accompanying angels (Gen. 18; cf. Gen. 19:1).

Abraham didn't realize that He was entertaining supernatural beings and that His hospitality to the Lord was really a sacrifice! The book of Hebrews makes a practical application: "Do not forget to entertain strangers, for by so doing some have unwittingly entertained angels" (Heb. 13:2). Jesus went a step further, declaring that anything that we do to help anyone is also for Him (Matt. 25:34-40).

The introduction to Numbers 15 indicates why these ritual instructions are here: "And the Lord spoke to Moses, saying, 'Speak to the children of Israel, and say to them: "When you have come into the land you are to inhabit, which I am giving to you . . ."'" (verses 1, 2). Coming as they do after the tragic story in the previous chapter, these words are full of encouragement, confirming that the Lord was still planning to give Canaan to the (younger generation of) Israelites. His grace was still available through sacrifices, which pointed to the ultimate Sacrifice of His Son (John 1:29).

More encouragement comes in another instruction that will go into effect when the Israelites enter the Promised Land and "eat of the bread of the land" (Num. 15:17-21). That is what they have been wanting to do! To remember their dependence on God and thank Him for His sustaining power (cf. Ps. 145:15, 16), they will offer Him a "donation" set aside from the first batch of dough that they make from the grain they harvest each year.

It is also encouraging to remember that if the Israelite community or an individual inadvertently/unwittingly violates any of the Lord's commands in the future, those sins can be removed and they can be forgiven (Num. 15:22-29; cf. Lev. 4). But then Numbers 15:30, 31 issues a powerful warning. In stark contrast to persons who commit inadvertent sins, defiant (literally "high-handed") sinners have no opportunity to receive forgiveness through animal sacrifice. Because they have reviled the Lord and despised His word, they bear their own blame and are "cut off," condemned to losing out on an afterlife. It is true that some deliberate sins could be forgiven through animal sacrifices (Lev. 5:1, 5, 6; 6:1-7), but not sins committed defiantly.

Coming after the rebellion following the report of the scouts (Num. 13; 14), the force of the warning is crystal clear: The younger generation should never sin defiantly, as the community of their parents had done! That kind of sin results in irrevocable punishment, with no ritual remedy available.

In case the Israelites needed an example of a defiant sin on the individual level, during their time in the wilderness a man worked by gathering pieces of wood on the Sabbath (Num. 15:32). His action was a flagrant violation of one of the Ten Commandments, which God Himself had proclaimed from Mount Sinai (Ex. 20:8-11) and repeated on other occasions (Ex. 23:12; 31:12-17; 34:21; 35:2, 3; see also Ex. 16:23-30). At the Lord's command the whole community stoned him to death (Num. 15:33-36).

The man represented the attitude of his generation. He had left Egypt, but Egypt had not left him. Although God had set him free, he was still acting like a slave of Pharaoh, gathering stuff (cf. Ex. 5:4-12) on the day that celebrated redemption, freedom from work, and dependence on the Creator who made and sustains all life (Ex. 20:8-11; Deut. 5:12-15; cf. Dan. 5:23).[1] By refusing to receive and celebrate the Lord's gift of life, he rejected God and chose the way of death. Ironically, the community that executed him consisted largely of the generation that he represented. In him they could see themselves.

So is there no hope for people who commit defiant sins? What about King Manasseh, the baddest of the bad, who perpetrated more than enough violence, idolatry, child sacrifice, and dabbling in the occult to richly deserve death and "cutting off" (2 Chron. 33; cf. Lev. 20:2, 3)? How did the Lord forgive him (2 Chron. 33:12, 13)? Talk about amazing grace!

Acts 13:39 gives the answer: Through the sacrifice of Christ, in which there alone exists real power for forgiveness (Heb. 10:1-18), there is opportunity to receive justification from sins for which the law of Moses (including the system of animal sacrifices) possessed no remedy. The ritual system, through which the Israelites obtained mercy by accepting Christ's sacrifice by faith, was to teach the people how salvation works. But it had limits.

Long ago the Lord told Moses that He could bear/forgive "transgression," that is, rebellious sin (Ex. 34:7), but not through animal sacrifice. It is true that the rebellious sins of God's professed people that affected His sanctuary (Lev. 20:3; Num. 19:13, 20; cf. Dan. 8:12), representing His reputation, were purged out on the Day of Atonement (Lev. 16:16; cf. Dan. 8:14). But the cleansing brought the rebellious sinners themselves no benefit (cf. Lev. 16:30; Dan. 8:25).

Everyone on Planet Earth in every age is saved the same way: through the gift of God's Son, "that *whoever* believes in Him should not perish but have everlasting life" (John 3:16). "Whoever" means "whoever," with no exceptions. The only ones shut out are those who ultimately refuse to believe. So even malicious, malignant Manasseh, when he believed, could, through the coming sacrifice of Christ, be snatched from a one-way ticket to certain hell. This does not mean that sinners can necessarily escape the consequences of their actions (perhaps even death) in the present life. Christ's promise of salvation is for the next life, which is eternal.

When we look out into the world at the people whom God wants to save, it is pretty scary. Take Ron Halverson, for instance. Ron grew up in a rough ghetto neighborhood of tenements in Brooklyn, New York City. In his high school, students killed each other with switchblade knives to get lunch money. At an early age he learned how to defend himself, and later he became a boxing champion, whom the press called "Killer Halverson." He also learned to "live by the order of the gun."

Ron's role models were tough—members of the Mafia and gangs. When he joined the Beach Combers gang, he stole cars and committed all kinds of other crimes by the time he was 16 years old. He saw friends die of wounds from sawed-off shotguns and served some time in jail. But that did not deter him. He worked his way up and became vice president of the Beach Combers.

Ron and a friend often skipped school to play pool (billiards). One school day, however, they decided to visit a buddy of theirs who had been placed in a Christian reform school up in Queens. When they arrived, they discovered that a Week of Prayer service was in progress. For the rest of the week they continued skipping school to attend the series of meetings. The speaker made an appeal at the end of the last meeting. Wearing a black leather jacket with his gang's emblem on the back, and with switchblades in his pockets, Ron walked to the front and gave his life to Christ. He figured that if Christ could save the thief on the cross, the Lord could save him, too. Today Ron Halverson is an internationally known evangelist.[2]

---

[1] For this insight I am grateful to my student Mathilde Frey, who is currently at Andrews University writing her Ph.D. in Religion dissertation, entitled "The Sabbath in the Pentateuch: An Exegetical and Theological Study."

[2] "From Gangs to God," sermon by Ron Halverson. http://www.wordoftruth radio.com/audio/view.php?speaker=6&sermon=71.

Chapter 7

CRISIS OVER LEADERSHIP
(Numbers 16; 17)

Mutiny

The year was 1842. The United States Navy was using the U.S.S. *Somers* as a training ship. The crew included several teenage midshipmen. The ship sailed to Africa, and then the captain, Commander Alexander Mackenzie, heard about a mutinous plot. The ringleader was acting midshipman Philip Spencer, the son of the secretary of war, John C. Spencer. He and two other sailors planned to seize the *Somers* and convert it into a pirate ship, killing anyone who got in their way.

A search of Spencer's cabin disclosed incriminating evidence, including a list of names, written in Greek, of crew members who would be retained after the mutiny, and a drawing of the *Somers* flying a pirate flag. A judicial panel unanimously found the sailors to be guilty. Three days later the crew hanged Spencer and his companions from the rigging of the ship. Thus ended the only instance of mutiny ever recorded in the history of the U.S. Navy.

Mutiny is rebellion against legal authority, especially by military personnel who refuse to obey orders and may attack their officers. It is a serious offense. In the United States conviction for such a crime can still result in capital punishment, while in the United Kingdom the penalty was death until 1998.[1]

The year was the second year after the Israelites left Egypt, on the continent of Africa.

They constituted an army, with the Lord as Commander-in-Chief and Moses and Aaron as His generals. Then one day Moses heard of a mutinous plot:

"Now Korah the son of Izhar, the son of Kohath, the son of Levi, with Dathan and Abiram the sons of Eliab, and On the son of Peleth, sons of Reuben, took men; and they rose up before Moses with some of the children of Israel, two hundred and fifty leaders of the congregation, representatives of the congregation, men of renown. They gathered together against Moses and Aaron, and said to them, 'You take too much upon yourselves, for all the congregation is holy, every one of them, and the Lord is among them. Why then do you exalt yourselves above the assembly of the Lord?'" (Num. 16:1, 2).

Thus begins one of the most dramatic, gut-wrenching episodes in the entire Bible. Here is no rash teenager and a couple of his foolish buddies trying to hijack a ship. It is a major coup attempt by a large, well-organized group of mature, experienced, intelligent leaders. In fact, they are almost guaranteed to succeed in hijacking the Israelite nation by triggering a revolution with overwhelming popular support. The reason is that Moses has told the adult generation that they are sentenced to death by wandering in the wilderness (Num. 14:26-39). From their point of view Moses and Aaron are the enemies, and the people are doomed anyway, so what do they have to lose? Highly motivated to get out from under their present leadership, they mutiny, but not for adventure and profit at sea, but for survival on land!

The argument against Moses and Aaron started off with the idea that all the Israelites were holy and that the Lord was among them. Indeed, it was true that God had called all the people to be "a kingdom of priests and a holy nation" (Ex. 19:6; cf. Lev. 11:44, 45; 19:2). In fact, tassels on the corners of their garments were to remind them that they were to be holy for Him (Num. 15:37-41). It was also true that the Lord was indeed among them. He had been trying to convince them to accept and respect the reality of His presence (cf. Ex. 17:7; Num. 11:20).

The punchline of Korah and company was: Moses and Aaron are

not showing respect to their holy people, but have concentrated too much power in themselves. Their argument echoed that of Miriam and Aaron against Moses: We are really all on a similar level, so what makes you think you are so special (Num. 12:2)? The obvious implication of the mutineers was: "Get off your high horse! Stop telling everyone what to do! Step down! Resign now!" They didn't stop to think about what had happened to Miriam (verse 10).

When Moses heard the fighting words, he fell on his face (Num. 16:4). He would have been devastated for several reasons:

1. The conflict after the scouting episode (Num. 14) should have been over, but here it was back again, worse than ever.

2. If Korah and his cohorts succeeded in hijacking the nation, would the younger generation also lose the Promised Land? Would Israel simply cease to exist?

3. Moses and Aaron had inducted the Levites, including Korah and the Levites who were with him, to their exalted role. In fact, Korah was closely related to Moses and Aaron (Kohathite Levite— Ex. 6:14-27; Num. 3:19). So this was betrayal on a colossal scale.

4. An attempted power grab of this nature is often lethal to the party that loses, because it often involves a fight to the death.

Moses was humble (cf. Num. 12:3), but he could defend the Lord's honor and respond to Korah's challenge to Aaron's leadership as high priest. So he got up from the ground and answered the conspirators. Korah and his Levite colleagues were already highly honored servants of God. But apparently regarding that as of little significance, they demanded a promotion to priesthood, where the real power resided. If they wanted to compete with Aaron and his sons for the job, they could show up for work the next day with priestly tools (censers with burning incense) and see if God would accept them (Num. 16:5-11)!

The challenge was simple and attractive, an offer that Korah and his company did not refuse. But they should have known that the priestly duel was deadly. Even though Nadab and Abihu had been sons of Aaron, they had died instantly when they offered incense before God (Lev. 10:1, 2). So how would the Levites fare if they got too close to His glorious presence? Not even authorized for priestly service, they didn't stand a chance! God had explicitly warned that any person attempting to usurp priestly function would be put to death (Num. 3:10, 38). The Levites were holy, but not chosen by God to be His priests. Without the asbestos suit of His special consecration (Lev. 8), they would be toast!

Then Moses summoned Dathan and Abiram of the tribe of Reuben. Unlike the opposition of Korah and other Levites who wanted Aaron's priesthood, the antagonism of Dathan and Abiram was almost exclusively directed against Moses'. They were bitter and refused to come, but sent a sizzling message directly summarizing the spirit of rebellion against Moses' leadership:

"Is it a small thing that you have brought us up out of a land flowing with milk and honey, to kill us in the wilderness, that you should keep acting like a prince over us? Moreover you have not brought us into a land flowing with milk and honey, nor given us inheritance of fields and vineyards. Will you put out the eyes of these men? We will not come up!" (Num. 16:13, 14).

Their accusation was utterly outrageous. Moses had never promised to bring the Israelites to Canaan all by himself. He had only put the Israelites in touch with God, whose leading and power alone could accomplish such an impossible task. The Israelites had rejected God's leading and were suffering the natural result. But they insisted on blaming Moses for everything and refused to take any responsibility for themselves.

Guy Cotter, a mountain guide who has reached the summit of Mount Everest three times, explains the respective roles of the guide and of those he leads:

"It's the client's responsibility to look after themselves. I mean, it's their life, they have to help us to help them. And that's something that we really reinforce with our clients. . . . A guide is somebody who is making the expedition happen for you and paving the path to the summit, if you like, but not carrying you up there, not dragging you up there. And if you're making mistakes, then that surely cannot in most situations be held as the guide's responsibility."[2]

The words of Dathan and Abiram, "Will you put out the eyes of these men?" were slanderous, falsely accusing Moses of being a

84

cruel tyrant. They echoed the spirit of a Hebrew slave who struck another Hebrew the day after Moses had killed an Egyptian to save a slave. When Moses asked why he was doing that, the man retorted: "Who made you a prince and a judge over us? Do you intend to kill me as you killed the Egyptian?" (Ex. 2:14). But if the Lord had not made Moses a prince and judge over the Israelites, they would still be slaves in Egypt.

Moses was so angry with Dathan and Abiram that he became an anti-intercessor. He asked the Lord to reject the two men by paying no heed to any offering that they would present to Him (Num. 16:15).

As Moses had instructed, the next day Korah and his group assembled at the sanctuary for the showdown with Moses and Aaron. Two hundred fifty rebels had censers with burning incense. Then the Lord's glory appeared to everyone (verses 16–19). This was ominous. Divine executive judgment was in session at God's sanctuary headquarters (cf. Num. 12:4, 5; 14:10).

The Lord did not discuss His plans with Moses and offer to make of him a great nation instead of the Israelites (contrast Num. 14:11, 12). Rather, He simply ordered Moses and Aaron to get out of the way so that He could instantly destroy the entire community. His fuse was very short. However, rather than run for cover, Moses and Aaron fell on their faces where they were and interceded for the community as a whole. Nevertheless, God insisted that they move away from the dwellings of the chief rebels (Num. 16:20–24). Although the rebels were in the Israelite camp, they had to be isolated so that harm would not fall on others.

Rather than taking care of his own safety, Moses went with the elders to warn the people who lived in the neighborhood of Dathan and Abiram to get away from their tents. Korah lived near the sanctuary (Num. 3:29), so the people there would have already heard the warning.

Dueling censers were about to settle the struggle between Korah and company and Aaron and his sons. But within view of the dwellings of Dathan and Abiram Moses announced the divine test of his own leadership, which would conclusively answer their accusations.

"By this you shall know that the Lord has sent me to do all these works, for I have not done them of my own will. If these men die naturally like all men, or if they are visited by the common fate of all men, then the Lord has not sent me. But if the Lord creates a new thing, and the earth opens its mouth and swallows them up with all that belongs to them, and they go down alive into the pit, then you will understand that these men have rejected the Lord" (Num. 16:28-30).

Of course, it was utterly impossible for Moses to trigger such an unprecedented, surgically precise geological phenomenon. If it happened, it would be a new kind of destructive miracle by the Creator-God. By consigning the rebels to the nether regions, the place of burial, the heavenly Lord of life would dramatically show that He had rejected them because they had spurned Him.

No one had time to ponder the chilling challenge. As though the earth was a giant living monster, it opened its gaping mouth under all the rebels, with their possessions and families, and swallowed them whole. Their screams vanished with a resounding thud as the earth closed over them (verses 31-33).

In trying to exalt themselves, they went down. Casting dirt on Moses, they had tons of it land on them. Moses didn't put out their eyes (verse 14)—the Lord put them out of sight. Having previously accepted the message that the Promised Land "devours its inhabitants" (Num. 13:32), they were literally devoured by the wilderness.

The Israelites witnessing the seismic execution thought they were next and fled in panic. Meanwhile, back at the sanctuary, divine fire consumed the 250 wannabe priests, as could have been expected (Num. 16:34, 35). It was all over in a few moments.

When the dust settled, the holy fire went out, and the mess was cleaned up, it appeared that the mutiny had been crushed. With a breathtaking display of justice and power, the Lord had annihilated the ringleaders. The 250 bronze censers had received holy fire, even though their unauthorized owners could not survive it. Therefore, the censers were holy and belonged to God at the sanctuary. The Lord directed that they be hammered into plating to cover the outside of the altar as a prominent, visible warning to any nonpriest tempted to share their fate in the future (verses 36-40).

The story of Korah, Dathan, and Abiram and their comrades is the classic demonstration of what the Lord thinks of rebellion against His true appointed leaders. He uses human beings to direct other people in carrying out His work in the world instead of appointing angels to do the job. True, His human leaders have their faults, but insofar as they discern and follow His will, they represent Him. So rebellion against their leadership is rejection of Him.

It is rather easy for those not bearing the heavy burdens of leadership to imagine that they could do a better job, especially if they possess robust egos and a desire to get ahead. Without understanding all the varied factors that affect God's work, one can suppose that solutions to problems are simpler than they are, and if only I were in charge, things would improve in a hurry. But it is discernment of the big picture that provides balanced perspective. When a crisis looms and things go wrong, it is natural to call for "change." But changing leaders is not always for the better.

It is easy for self-appointed leaders, including those who manipulate authorized avenues to gain and hold on to positions of legitimate authority, to claim that they follow in the sandal prints of Moses and Aaron as the Lord's authorized representatives. Yet they are more faithful to themselves and their own interests than to God's gospel mission agenda, with its sacred task of delivering as many people as possible safely to the Promised Land. Permitting no opposition to their proud, selfish wills, they cite the story of Korah, Dathan, and Abiram to defend their leadership, and self-righteously intone: "Do not stretch out your hand against the Lord's anointed" (see 1 Sam. 24:6, 10; 26:9, 11, 23; 2 Sam. 1:14, 16). But the heritage of their leadership is that of Korah and the others who attempted to usurp the place of Moses and Aaron and hijack Israel.

Between the Living and the Dead

My wife and I climbed Mount Lassen, a volcanic peak in northern California, when our daughter was less than 2 years old. So I carried Sarah in a backpack. Unfortunately, she did not enjoy the experience, because she strongly objected to the powerful and noisy wind that swept across our trail. To play a game with her that would

87

hopefully cheer her up, we stepped behind a big boulder that blocked the wind, and I commanded: "Wind, stop!" Sure enough, the wind momentarily abated until we passed by the rock.

My plan backfired. Sarah thought I could stop the wind and should do so all the time. So she kept insisting, with a very definite tone of voice: "Daddy, wind 'top!" Of course, the mountain wind was beyond my control, so I did not even attempt to exert my will over its robust gusts. When I failed to say the magic words and thus did nothing about the unpleasant situation, Sarah was angry with me. So loud wails accompanied our hike up Lassen Peak.

The children of Israel also blamed their leaders for something beyond the latter's control. The day after Korah and his colleagues died, the whole Israelite community blamed Moses and Aaron for killing the rebels, whom they called "the people of the Lord" (Num. 16:41)! Here was full-scale revolution! Rather than a couple hundred rebels, now many thousands shared the spirit of Korah and his companions and refused to recognize God's role, in spite of the miraculous nature of events. Had the ground gulped down whole families by the power of Moses? Had Aaron lit the fire that fried 250 men?

Again, the glory of the Lord appeared. And again the Lord issued the order to get away so that He could instantly consume the Israelites. Because they were with Korah and company, they would share their fate (cf. verses 19-21). Once more Moses and Aaron fell on their faces (verses 42-45; cf. verses 19-22). But now they could no longer defend the people by pleading that God should limit His retribution to certain rebel leaders (cf. verses 22-24). The Israelites had destroyed any arguments that intercessors might use on their behalf.

The Lord had no fuse left. Moses knew this was it! As soon as the fatal decree had left the divine lips (which had spoken the world into existence) a lethal plague shot into the community to ravage the Israelite nation into nonexistence. People were already dying.

Without immediate atonement, the Israelites would all perish. There was no time to offer a sacrifice, and atonement needed to go out and reach them where they were. So Moses told Aaron, the high priest, to grab a censer, burn incense, and quickly take it to the people in order to make atonement for them. The sprightly octogenarian (now in his mid–80s [Ex. 7:7]) ran in order to save as many as possible (Num. 16:46, 47). Where his intercessory incense reached, people lived. Where it did not, they died. "And he stood between the dead and the living; so the plague was stopped" (verse 48).

For 14,700 it was too late (verse 49). All the others had only the compassion and quick reaction of Moses and Aaron and the mercy of God to thank for their survival. For malicious false witness against Moses and Aaron, whom they had slanderously accused of murder, the Israelites deserved to suffer capital punishment for murder (cf. Deut. 19:16-19). But the very ones they had so viciously wronged had saved their lives, saying, in effect, "Father, forgive them, for they do not know what they do" (Luke 23:34). And by accepting the ritual intercession of Aaron, the mediator whom He had appointed, the Lord showed astounding grace.

According to Peter, Christians belong to the Lord as "a royal priesthood" (1 Peter 2:9). One of the main functions of a priesthood is to mediate for people. God does not ask us to do it by carrying censers, as Aaron did, but to pray with the assistance of a mediator in heaven: "Then another angel, having a golden censer, came and stood at the altar. He was given much incense, that he should offer it with the prayers of all the saints upon the golden altar which was before the throne" (Rev. 8:3).

Just as the intercession of Moses and Aaron made a huge difference, our intercessory prayers affect the salvation of others. Where intercession reaches, empowered by the heavenly incense of God's love through Christ, people who would otherwise die live. We too stand between the living and the dead.

Proof of Priesthood

The Israelites had received miraculous evidence that the Lord had chosen only Aaron and his sons for the priesthood. Others had perished by divine fire while offering incense, but Aaron and his sons had survived. Not only that, God's recognition of Aaron's incense had protected the nation.

After the terrifying plague, the Lord wanted to reinforce His choice of Aaron's family for the priesthood even more, this time by a positive display of His creative power. So He instructed Moses to set up a test with wooden staffs from the chieftains representing the 12 tribes. Aaron's staff would depict the tribe of Levi. Each man's staff symbolized his identity (cf. Gen. 38:18), and Moses also wrote their names on their staffs. God would cause the dead wood of the staff belonging to the man chosen for priesthood to blossom miraculously. In this clear way He planned to put to rest permanently any remaining doubts about the exclusive authority of the Aaronic priesthood (Num. 17:1-5).

Moses placed the staffs before the Lord in the sanctuary. The very next day Aaron's staff had not only blossomed but yielded ripe almonds. Moses showed the people all the staffs so they could see the evidence for themselves. Then he put Aaron's staff back in the sanctuary in front of the Testimony, that is, in front of the ark containing the Ten Commandments, which comprised the covenant testimony or witness between the Lord and the Israelites. The special staff would serve as a permanent sign to settle any question about the right of Aaron and his descendants to worship leadership over Israel (verses 6-11). By controlling the priesthood, the Lord regulated Israelite worship. It would protect the Israelites from falling into worship practices that would misrepresent Him in the world.

Everything is clear except for one thing: Why did God choose to make Aaron's staff blossom and produce almonds? For one thing, a golden blossom or rosette, engraved with the words "Holiness to the Lord," decorated the front of the headdress of the high priest (Ex. 28:36; 39:30). Furthermore, the candleholders of the lampstand in the sanctuary had the shape of almond blossoms (Ex. 25:33, 34; 37:19, 20). So there were strong connections between the miracle and what it meant: Aaron would serve as high priest at the sanctuary.

And there is one more detail. The Hebrew word for "almonds" comes from a root that means "to watch" or "keep watch." In the Near Middle East almond trees are the first trees to blossom every year. So people have come to regard them as "watchful ones." This connection between almonds and watching explains an object lesson the Lord gave to young Jeremiah: "The word of the Lord came to me, saying, 'Jeremiah, what do you see?' And I said, 'I see a branch of an almond tree.' Then the Lord said to me, 'You have seen well, for I am watching over my word to perform it' " (Jer. 1:11, 12, NRSV).

Now we can understand the symbolism of the almond blossoms on the lampstand, which provided light all night to show that the Lord was always watching over His people (Ps. 121:4; cf. Ps. 127:1). We can also recognize the implied warning in the almonds on Aaron's staff: The Lord would be watchful to guard Aaron's priest-hood, as He explicitly warned: "Put back Aaron's staff in front of the Testimony, to be kept as a sign to the rebellious. This will put an end to their grumbling against me, so that they will not die" (Num. 17:10, NIV).

[1] http://militaryhistory.suite101.com/article.cfm/uss_somers_mutiny_1842; http://en.wikipedia.org/wiki/Mutiny#United_Kingdom.
[2] http://www.pbs.org/wgbh/pages/frontline/everest/stories/leadership.html.

Chapter 8

COPING WITH DANGER AND DEATH

(Numbers 18; 19)

The Lord's "Nuclear Reactor"

Many years ago a farmer in Minnesota took his wheat to a grain silo. During the trip he walked next to his horse as it pulled the cart. When they had almost arrived, the plodding horse looked up and saw the silo. At that moment a freak tornado scooped up the horse and cart and deposited them some distance away. The poor animal was un-harmed but understandably traumatized, and the grain was gone.

The next year the same farmer used the same horse and cart to transport another load of wheat to the same silo. When they had almost arrived, the horse glanced up and saw the silo. Remembering what had happened to him the last time he was there, he jerked around and galloped away as fast as his hooves would carry him. No way was he going through that again!

The Israelites had seen the Lord's terrible swift sword on a num-ber of occasions, but this last time had been a very close call for all of them, and the body count was high (14,700). No way did they want to go through that again! "So the children of Israel spoke to Moses, saying, 'Surely we die, we perish, we all perish! Whoever even comes near the tabernacle of the Lord must die. Shall we all ut-terly die?'" (Num. 17:12, 13).

The adult generation of Israelites were condemned to die in the wilderness (Num. 14), but at least that was a natural death. Now they feared that they had so severely offended the Lord that they would not even be safe getting close to Him by bringing offerings to His sanctuary. Of course, they had found themselves in so much trouble not because they had exercised their legitimate privilege of coming to the sanctuary courtyard to present sacrifices, but because of their rebellion.

The Lord understood, and provided a new rule of engagement to calm the fear of the people: "The Lord said to Aaron: You and your sons and your ancestral house with you shall bear responsibility for offenses connected with the sanctuary, while you and your sons alone shall bear responsibility for offenses connected with the priesthood" (Num. 18:1, NRSV). It meant that if a nonpriest made a mistake at the sanctuary, the priests, as the mediators and representatives of the Israelites, would bear the responsibility. But no longer would such a situation result in the Lord's retribution breaking out on the whole community (cf. Num. 16:19-21, 41-49).

As the Lord had specified before, the Levites were to assist the priests (cf. Num. 8). But if Levites tried to act as priests, as Korah and his companions had done (Num. 16), both they and at least some priests would die (Num. 18:2-7). To protect themselves from God's wrath, the highly motivated priestly guards of the holy domain (armed with weapons—see Numbers 25:7) received the authority to put to death anyone, including a Levite, who attempted to usurp priestly function at the sanctuary. So it would never again be necessary to have a duel of censers (Num. 16). Any anti-priestly rebellion, which could jeopardize communal safety, would be swiftly nipped in the bud.

Killing trespassers in their tracks may appear extreme and "un-Christian" until we remember the awesomeness of the Lord. He creates worlds from nothing and wings new galaxies and nebulas out into space as if they were Frisbees. God can impose His will on trillions of tons of matter by merely speaking (Gen. 1). His glory is a consuming fire (Ex. 24:17; Deut. 4:24; 9:3; Heb. 12:29). So when He resided at the Israelite sanctuary, the power concentrated there made it like a nuclear reactor. There had to be special safeguards for the surrounding community to survive.

One fine day, Chris (17 years old) and his buddies were looking for adventure and decided to explore the shore of Lake Michigan. Walking about a mile from Grand Mere beach, they came to a sign that read "No Trespassing. Violators Will Be Prosecuted." So they realized that they had arrived at the Cook Nuclear Power Plant. Assuming that the sign prohibited access only by land, they decided to go around on the water. They had an inflatable raft for two, and the third had a skimboard.

After a half hour of paddling in the water, the teenagers were only halfway around the nuclear plant and were already tiring. Suddenly the boy on the skimboard jumped into the raft in alarm because the water was churning, bubbling, and warm like a hot tub. They needed to get out of there! Then they saw a Coast Guard boat approaching and were relieved to be picked up.

The crew of the boat sternly informed Chris and his friends that they had been in a restricted zone, and it was surprising that they had not been drowned by the great sucking action from the cooling process of the nearby plant. Later their parents learned that snipers at the plant had been watching them, but had decided that the teenagers did not look dangerous enough to gun down!

It makes good sense to defend a nuclear power plant from unauthorized individuals in order to protect people living nearby (including my nuclear family!). How much more important it was to guard the sanctuary, in which the infinitely greater power of the Lord resided! He could control His power, of course, but He wanted the Israelites to respect His greatness so that they would trust in His ability to help and deliver them.

Today we do not have the Shekinah presence of God dwelling in an earthly sanctuary/Temple. So we do not need to guard our churches with weapons in order to keep people out. However, it is still important to protect reverently the Lord's moral boundaries of holiness in His church. When a member of the church of Corinth was living in open sin with his stepmother, which defamed Christ's holy reputation in that city (1 Cor. 5:1), Paul commanded that the church community remove him from membership: "In the name of our Lord Jesus Christ, when you are gathered together, along with my spirit, with the power of our Lord Jesus Christ, deliver such a one to Satan for the destruction of the flesh, that his spirit may be saved in the day of the Lord Jesus" (verses 4, 5).

Under the Old Testament theocracy, removal of such a person from the community was more drastic and permanent. For example, "the man who lies with his father's wife has uncovered his father's nakedness; both of them shall surely be put to death. Their blood shall be upon them" (Lev. 20:11). Now we have a church, not a nation, so disfellowshipping applies to cases that would have required the death penalty in Old Testament law.

Many Christians today are completely unwilling to protect the boundaries of God's holiness. In the name of Christian "love," a spineless feeling consisting of mercy uncomplicated by justice, anything goes. Several years ago a pastor told me that when he began work in a particular congregation, he encountered a need for church discipline in a clear case of open sin that called for removal from membership. But existing memory had no record of such discipline ever being carried out. So when the pastor presented the case at a church business meeting, the members refused to support his recommendation that the church drop the guilty parties from membership.

Unbridled mercy at the expense of justice hurts God's holy cause in the world. It injures people too. When there is no accountability, people think that things are OK, and that there is peace when there is none (Jer. 6:14; 8:11). Such an approach endangers their eternal salvation. Paul made it clear that it is far better, and potentially redemptive, to recognize a crisis and hopefully wake up a guilty person by delivering "such a one to Satan for the destruction of the flesh, that his spirit may be saved" (1 Cor. 5:5).

Unbridled mercy that allows destructive behaviors also damages innocent victims. They include children of parents who are divorced because of an extramarital affair that may not have happened if the church had upheld its moral standards. Others victims suffer from sexual molestation, slander, financial oppression, and so on. The list is endless. Known offenders get let off the hook to strike again, or they simply transfer to other church communities, where they can do their thing all over again. Congregations may write letters and hold meetings about the situation, but nothing changes. Doesn't anyone have the guts to put a stop to this?

We have found that the story of God's dealings with ancient

Israel recorded in the book of Numbers lavishly illustrates the fact that there is such a thing as corporate responsibility. The community of God's people is accountable to Him for supporting the Lord's leaders in guarding His holiness in the world. Unfortunately, many modern church communities are failing miserably, with family lifestyle statistics no better than those of the surrounding ungodly "civilization." As Paul told the Corinthians, it is high time for those who are called as God's "holy ones" to start living up to their name (1 Cor. 1, etc.).

Compensation for Hazardous Duty

Highly trained personnel serving in hazardous duty to benefit and protect an entire community should receive good compensation. So as a permanent agreement ("covenant of salt"), the Lord assigned to the Israelite priests a fine source of income from portions of the offerings that the people brought to Him (Num. 18:8-19).

As assistants of the priests, the Levites also participated in dangerous duty on behalf of the Israelites (verses 22, 23; cf. Num. 8:19), although it was less perilous than priestly work. The entire tribe of Levi, including the priests, would not have an inheritance of territory from which to make an agricultural living. Rather, their support came from serving God: Israelites were to give their tithes (one tenth of their agricultural increase; cf. Deut. 14:22) to the Levites, who in turn would pass on a tenth to the priests (Num. 18:20-32).

By giving the priests and Levites a good, regular income, the Lord made it unnecessary for them to "moonlight." They could easily devote all their time and energy to His service.

When Christ sent out 70 disciples, He affirmed that those dedicated to His work for the benefit of others deserve material support: "And remain in the same house, eating and drinking such things as they give, for the laborer is worthy of his wages" (Luke 10:7). Paul applied the same principle: "Do you not know that those who minister the holy things eat of the things of the temple, and those who serve at the altar partake of the offerings of the altar? Even so the Lord has commanded that those who preach the gospel should live from the gospel" (1 Cor. 9:13, 14).

Today we have no Levites or ritual priesthood. Nor do most of us make our living by farming, so we have no agricultural tithes to present to God for His workers. Nevertheless, an adapted system of tithing is a practical way to support individuals so that they can devote themselves exclusively to the Lord's work.

As a widow discovered when she fed Elijah, the Lord does not allow those who generously support His ministers to miss what they give (1 Kings 17:8-16). Rather, their faith in His ability to provide and their dedication to His mission lets Him lavish His blessings upon them: " ' Bring all the tithes into the storehouse, that there may be food in My house, and try Me now in this,' says the Lord of hosts, 'if I will not open for you the windows of heaven and pour out for you such blessing that there will not be room enough to receive it' " (Mal. 3:10).

So what if God's ministers are not using sacred tithes and offerings as well as they should? For that they are accountable to Him and His church. But such a situation does not diminish the blessing for a member who faithfully entrusts to the Lord what is His.

Provision for Future Purification

My wife, Connie, teaches archaeology at the Seventh-day Adventist Theological Seminary at Andrews University. She recently served as coleader of a study tour in Egypt, taking care of many practical details. One involved helping keep students and faculty members (including me) as healthy as possible. This is still a challenge in Egypt (cf. Ex. 15:26).

Sure enough, at one point in the trip, a number of tour participants developed varieties of a condition that tourists commonly call King Tut's revenge (equivalent to the American Montezuma's revenge). Aside from faintness and nausea, another effect of this sickness makes it highly inconvenient to travel in areas of limited toilet facilities.

To remedy the situation, Connie asked our bus to stop by a pharmacy. She went in and bought out much of the store's stock of the medicine that our group needed. Emerging with arms full of small packages, she was able to supply everyone who was sick. As a result, each one quickly came down with a case of good health, and the tour proceeded successfully, without interruption.

When you have a lot of people, you need a major supply. Or when you want a batch to last for a long time, you make a big one. That's what the Israelites did when they needed to treat the physical ritual impurity of corpse contamination. Under the direction of a priest, they made a big batch of sacrificial ashes that would last for a long time. Later they added water to some of the ashes and sprinkled the mixture on persons and things contaminated by contact with or proximity to dead bodies (Num. 19).

Back in Numbers 8 we already encountered "water of purification," which freed the Levites from corpse contamination (verse 7). But the directions for producing the ash-water mixture appear in Numbers 19. This makes sense in light of the development of the story, which has recently involved a lot of dead bodies (Num. 14; 16; 17).

The procedure for obtaining the ashes was a special kind of purification offering (a so-called sin offering [Num. 19:9]) of a reddish cow/heifer, which had the purpose of making it possible to purify persons and objects from physical ritual impurity. The New Revised Standard Version correctly translates "a purification offering" here, but the KJV, RSV, NKJV, NASB, and NIV incorrectly render it "purification/purifying from/for sin." Such mistranslations indicate that incurring corpse contamination itself was an act of sin, that is, violation of a divine commandment, which it was not (except for priests in forbidden cases [see Lev. 21]).

Physical ritual impurities, such as corpse contamination, scaly skin disease, and genital discharges, happened through physical processes often without human choice (see also Lev. 12-15). So confusing categories to make sin the same as physical ritual impurity yields the wrong implication that sins just automatically happen all the time and we can do nothing about that. Thus the great preacher Charles Spurgeon misinterpreted the red cow ritual: "Who has lived for a single day in this base world without discovering that in all his actions he commits sin, in everything to which he puts his hand, he receives, as well as imparts, some degree of defilement?"* Even inadvertent sins involve choices, although those who commit them do not realize until later that they have violated God's commands (Lev. 4).

If we suppose that we are simply sinning all the time, the way we breathe, we will lose our biblically balanced perspective. On the one hand, we can sink into despair and spend all our time confessing, as Martin Luther did before he understood the gospel. Alternatively, we can try to cope by at least partly giving up on accountability for our actions, so that cheap grace fictitiously accounts us righteous in heaven in spite of our true spiritual condition on earth.

Neither extreme is necessary. Sin is not automatic like involuntary physical processes, even though sins can become habits. When we commit a mistake of a kind that violates a divine command, we are accountable when we understand that our choice has broken God's law (Lev. 4:27, 28; cf. James 4:17). At that point the Lord gives us the opportunity to confess in order to receive forgiveness through the advocacy of Christ, whose sacrifice is for all of us (1 John 1:9–2:2).

The details of slaughtering and burning the red cow (Num. 19:1–10) suited its function.

Although it was a purification offering, it was performed outside the camp to spare the sanctuary from the intensity of the impurity that it remedied. Because it was a sacrifice, a priest had to officiate. He sprinkled blood toward the sanctuary (verse 4) to establish a connection to the usual place of sacrifice.

The victim was a cow, the largest female sacrificial animal. Purification offerings for the benefit of ordinary, individual Israelites were female animals (Lev. 4:28, 32; 5:6; Num. 15:27). It required a large animal to supply a lot of ashes that could be apportioned in small amounts to individuals of the entire community during a long period of time. The Israelites would increase the quantity of ashes by the addition of cedar wood (Num. 19:6).

Aromatic cedar wood was appropriate for purification, especially because it can be reddish, and red is the color of blood. The reddish color of the cow and the crimson yarn also added to the fire (verse 6) enhanced the association with blood. The ashes would function like dehydrated blood, to which water would later be added in order to reconstitute it as a liquid that could be sprinkled like blood (verses 12, 13, 17–20).

One aspect of the unique red cow ritual has especially perplexed interpreters of this passage: The (pure) participants in the burning of the cow and storing its ashes, as well as the pure person who later sprinkled the ash-water, all became impure because of these roles (verses 7, 8, 10, 21). Conversely, the ash-water purified those who were impure (verses 12, 19). Why would the same substance have such opposite effects on people?

The answer is that Israelites regarded the cow as a unit, both in space and time. So what happened to parts of it later—application of small portions of ashes on impure persons and things—they viewed as having already happened when the burning of the cow took place.

Therefore, the ashes absorbed impurity from impure individuals and objects, so that when a pure person touched the ashes or was involved in their production, that person received contamination from the ashes.

Compare this situation: If a dirty person takes a bath and becomes clean, and then a clean person gets in the water that's carrying the dirt from the first person, the clean person becomes dirty. The difference is that in the red cow ritual, a clean person would become impure even before the purifying substance contacted that which was impure. It would be like a clean individual becoming unclean by touching water in which a dirty person would later bathe.

This looks strange, but remember that the symbolic world of ritual does not depend on limitations of physical cause and effect. It points to a greater reality, and because it is a sacrifice, it points to Christ's sacrifice.

Only the red cow ritual highlighted the fact that Christ's sacrifice would supply the means of purification for many people who would need it after the cross event. That includes us! We were not even born until long after Jesus died on the cross. So how can we receive eternal life through what He did then?

The answer is that at the cross Christ made ample provision for everyone, and then He distributes the benefit to us through His high priestly ministry in heaven. Whereas the ashes of the red cow remedied only physical ritual impurity in the present life, Christ's blood provides moral purification for eternal life:

"For if the blood of goats and bulls, with the sprinkling of the ashes of a heifer, sanctifies those who have been defiled so that their flesh is purified, how much more will the blood of Christ, who through the eternal Spirit offered himself without blemish to God, purify our conscience from dead works to worship the living God!" (Heb. 9:13, 14, NRSV).

The red cow ritual, which purified the impure through the service of those who became impure as a result, reveals another profound aspect of Christ's sacrifice: "For He made Him who knew no sin to be sin for us, that we might become the righteousness of God in Him" (2 Cor. 5:21).

---

*Charles H. Spurgeon, *The Treasury of the Old Testament* (Grand Rapids: Zondervan, 1951), vol. 1, p. 359. It is true that in an extended sense the key aspects of this sacrifice teach us about Christ's redemption from all pollution, including that which results from committing sins. Recognizing that this is an extended sense helps us to avoid confusion of categories by which the "automatic" aspect of physical ritual impurity gets incorrectly carried over to committing sins.

Chapter 9

FAILURE AND SUCCESS
(Numbers 20; 21)

The Power of Mercy

After Numbers 19 provides instructions for treatment of corpse contamination, chapter 20 recounts more deaths. This time it is not large numbers of the community who perish, but Miriam and Aaron. Moses remains alive, but he too is condemned to die before the Israelites enter the Promised Land. Of the adults who left Egypt, only Caleb and Joshua would make it all the way to Canaan (see Num. 14:30; 26:65).

Miriam died first (Num. 20:1). The Bible does not state the reason she was not permitted to enter the Promised Land. Perhaps it was because of her disloyalty back at Hazeroth (Num. 12).

Soon after her death the Israelites blamed Moses and Aaron, especially Moses, for lack of water (Num. 20:2). It was similar to what had happened at Rephidim, before they had reached Mount Sinai. There they had questioned whether the Lord was among them or not, but He had shown His presence by causing water to come from a rock immediately after Moses struck it with his rod (Ex. 17:1-7).

This time the people added an ugly edge to their contention, saying: "If only we had died when our brethren died before the Lord! Why have you brought up the assembly of the Lord into this wilderness, that we and our animals should die here? And why have you made us come up out of Egypt, to bring us to this evil place? It is not a place of grain or figs or vines or pomegranates; nor is there any water to drink" (Num. 20:3–5).

They had learned nothing about faith, but wished that they had shared the fate of Korah, Dathan, Abiram, and the other rebels (Num. 16; 17)! In fact, their words echo the bitter attitude of Dathan and Abiram (Num. 16:13, 14).

Distraught and not knowing what to do, Moses and Aaron went to the sanctuary and fell on their faces. Then the Lord's glory appeared (Num. 20:6), as on previous occasions of rebellion (Num. 14:10; 16:19, 42). This was ominous, coming as it did after the escalation of divine punishments recorded earlier in the book of Numbers, which almost culminated in the annihilation of the nation (Num. 11; 14; 16). Had divine mercy on Israel finally run out?

What happened this time was much more surprising than destruction of many or even all of the people, something that we would expect as fully deserved. When the Lord appeared to Moses and Aaron, He told them to take "the rod," gather the community, and speak to a rock. As a result, the rock would miraculously release water to supply all the people and their livestock (Num. 20:7, 8).

That's all? No punishment on the people whatsoever? Just a repetition of the miracle at Rephidim? Pure mercy, repaying evil with good? What sense does that make? Precisely. Max Lucado has written: "I've never been surprised by God's judgment, but I'm still stunned by his grace. God's judgment has never been a problem for me. In fact, it always seemed right. Lightning bolts on Sodom. Fire on Gomorrah. Good job, God! Egyptians swallowed in the Red Sea. They had it coming. Forty years of wandering to loosen the stiff necks of the Israelites? Would've done it myself. Ananias and Sapphira? You bet.

"Discipline is easy for me to swallow. Logical to assimilate. Manageable and appropriate. But God's grace? Anything but."[1]

We love to sing "Amazing Grace," but do we take it for granted? What makes grace amazing is the fact that it is undeserved and therefore unexpected. Why does God give it? For one thing, mercy is an integral part of His loving character (Ex. 34:6, 7). And for another, mercy can be a powerful tool of "tough love" to break the resistance of stubborn hearts: "Beloved, do not avenge your-selves, but rather give place to wrath; for it is written, 'Vengeance is Mine, I will repay,' says the Lord. Therefore 'if your enemy is hun-gry, feed him; if he is thirsty, give him a drink; for in so doing you will heap coals of fire on his head.' Do not be overcome by evil, but overcome evil with good" (Rom. 12:19-21).

The Lord had given the Israelites ample demonstration of the fact that He has the right and power to carry out vengeance. Now that they understood this, He returned to the pre-Sinai approach of countering the people's antagonistic attitude by unexpectedly treat-ing them with kindness. Furthermore, He now focused on teaching the younger generation, who needed to understand His grace.

God's approach of punishing enemies with kindness, designed to make them ashamed of their obnoxious behavior, still works today. Some time ago a Jewish cantor (a singing worship leader) and his wife, who lived in Lincoln, Nebraska, were victims of obscene, anti-Semitic phone calls. The calls came from a wizard (leader) of the racist organization Ku Klux Klan. The couple did some investigation to find out who was expressing hatred toward them in this way. In the process they discovered that the nasty caller, whom they had never met, was disabled and could not easily go out to buy groceries.

The Jewish couple prepared a delicious meal for the KKK wiz-ard and took it to his house. When he opened the door, he was so flabbergasted that he invited them in. They kept coming back, and he gratefully accepted their friendship. Rather than seeking to de-stroy him, they had eradicated his toxic attitude.

This story is not an isolated case. George Wallace, the governor of Alabama, tried to block the civil rights movement in the United States. The gun of an attempted assassin put an end to his political career by incapacitating him. Toward the end of his life, when he could not take care of himself, the Black man who assisted him treated him with such tender kindness that he renounced his racism. Prejudice simply could not survive in such a loving atmosphere.

Of course, everyone has free choice. Some will ungratefully and illogically insist on being our enemies no matter what we do. But having done our part, and having prayed "Father, forgive them, for they do not know what they are doing" (Luke 23:34, NRSV), we can entrust them to the Lord of mercy and justice. We do not need to take upon ourselves the responsibility of making sure that the vengeance of retributive justice gets carried out. God can do a much more thorough job than we ever could.

Miracle and Mistake

"So Moses took the rod from before the Lord as He commanded him" (Num. 20:9). It was Moses' own staff (verse 11), not the one belonging to Aaron that had blossomed and yielded almonds, and that Moses had deposited at the sanctuary (Num. 17).

Moses' staff, which he must have also kept at the sanctuary "before the Lord," was the one that God had used as the instrument of wonders in Egypt, His deliverance from Pharaoh's army at the Red Sea, the miracle of water from the rock at Rephidim, and the victory over the Amalekites (Ex. 4; 7-10; 14; 17).

The staff of Moses represented his identity (cf. Gen. 38:18). If he were a king, it would have been his scepter, signifying his authority and power. However, Moses spoke of it as "the rod of God" (Ex. 17:9). It belonged to Moses, but he belonged to God. When Moses appeared before the Israelites with that remarkable staff, they received the strong impression that something awesome was about to happen. Would he strike a rock to give them water again, or would he strike them dead?

This time God wanted Moses and Aaron simply to speak to a designated rock, while Moses held the rod as a reminder of what the Lord had done in the past (Num. 20:8). By involving Aaron in the miracle, the Lord would once again affirm the leadership of the Aaronic priesthood, which the people would need to follow in the future. Speaking rather than striking would be a miracle even greater than the one at Rephidim. It was theoretically possible that when Moses had struck the rock there (Ex. 17:6), the blow had shattered a crust plugging an underground spring. If so, it could be argued that the miracle would have been to hit in precisely the right place. Speaking, however, could not possibly have any physical effect without the Lord directly intervening to move physical material.

Moses had been incredibly humble, patient, and forgiving in regard to all these people. Twice he had refused God's offer to make of him a great nation instead of them (Ex. 32:10-13; Num. 14:12-19). He had even interceded by asking that God blot his name out of the divine book if the Lord would not forgive them (Ex. 32:32). Now Moses stood in front of the rock with his staff in his hand, looking out over the Israelite community that had repeatedly rejected their gracious Lord and thwarted His glorious plans for them. Memories of their accumulated selfishness, stupidity, ingratitude, and treachery overwhelmed the great leader.

Suddenly he lost it and lashed out: " 'Hear now, you rebels! Must we bring water for you out of this rock?' Then Moses lifted his hand and struck the rock twice with his rod; and water came out abundantly, and the congregation and their animals drank" (Num. 20:10, 11).

The miracle happened, all right, and it solved the practical problem of water. But it was not the wonder that God had intended, which would have glorified Him as a result of the full trust of Moses and Aaron. Rather than speaking, Moses smashed the rock not just once but twice. Aaron did not participate in the miracle. Even worse, what happened did not convey God's message of mercy to the people. Moses did not even give the Lord credit. He, along with Aaron, had failed to carry out God's wishes as His servants and to represent Him as holy before the people.

Therefore, the Lord said that they could not lead the Israelites into the Promised Land (verse 12). They would die in the wilderness along with the unfaithful adult generation that had left Egypt. The language of Numbers 20:11 implies the seriousness of Moses' offense: "Moses lifted his hand" to strike the rock. This is the language of a "high-handed" or defiant sin, for which animal sacrifice provides no remedy (Num. 15:30, 31). Although Moses pleaded with the Lord to let him enter Canaan, the divine sentence was final (Deut. 3:23-27).

Aaron died first, in the fortieth year after the Israelites left Egypt, at the age of 123 (Num. 33:38, 39). In spite of his failure, God honored him by calling him up a mountain to die, closer to Himself. Before Aaron's death, Moses transferred his brother's high-priestly garments to Eleazar, the high priest's son, thus preventing the sacred vestments from becoming contaminated by Aaron's dead body. When Moses and Eleazar came down the mountain without Aaron, the Israelites mourned for 30 days (Num. 20:23-29). The month-long period gave them ample opportunity to reflect. They should have been dead, but instead, their priestly intercessor had perished.

Aaron was Israel's first high priest, and Moses was closer to God than any human being in history (Num. 12:7, 8; Deut. 34:10), except for Christ. The fact that God did not spare even Moses and Aaron when they violated their sacred trust is sobering to all Christians, and especially to leaders of God's work. There is never any excuse for deviating from the path that the Lord lays out for us, and the greater our privilege, responsibility, and influence, the greater our accountability.

When I was doing construction work in California to support my studies, I learned the difference between a highly paid carpenter and a laborer like me: The former is responsible for things that are much more expensive to fix if he does them wrong. Of course, a national leader can make mistakes millions of times more costly than those of a carpenter, as history lavishly illustrates. That is what Moses was: a national leader. The way he represented God to the people had a huge impact on their faith, which they desperately needed if their nation would even survive.

Even if we are not leaders like that, our influence affects the faith of others, which they must have if they are to be saved by God's grace (Eph. 2:8, 9). Do we think about that? Do we seize opportunities to build faith by praising God for what He is doing for us, or do we complain, as if He is not with us? When we face a problem, do we try to solve it on our own, or do we invite others to seek the Lord in prayer because the burden of leadership "will rest on His shoulders" (Isa. 9:6, NASB)?

Do we raise questions in immature minds, without giving answers, so that those who hear us become agnostic? After experiencing a couple years of such teaching, a relative of mine studying at a "Christian college" as a theology major didn't know whether he believed in God anymore. Or do we show how to develop a firm framework of faith, within which thinking people can process inevitable doubts and questions that may or may not be resolved before the second coming of Christ (cf. Deut. 29:29)?

In a sense, we live our lives standing before the rock with Moses! Let us tightly grip the staff that reminds us of what God has done for us in the past while we listen for what He wants us to speak so that others can receive His "water of life" through Christ (John 7:37, 38). The water does not come from us, but from Christ: "And all drank the same spiritual drink, for they were drinking from a spiritual rock which followed them; and the rock was Christ" (1 Cor. 10:4, NASB).

The New Testament explanation that the rock represents Christ raises an important point: To provide life-giving water, God only commanded Moses to strike the rock once—at Rephidim (Ex. 17:6). This correlates with the fact that in order to provide ultimate life, "Christ was offered once to bear the sins of many" (Heb. 9:28). From then on, we only need to speak to Him in order to receive life.

Holy War

A man driving along in the United States picked up a teenage hitchhiker. After a few miles, the boy pulled out a knife and demanded the man's wallet. The driver calmly replied, "Charlie won't like that." Puzzled, the boy brandished the knife a bit closer to the man and insisted: "Give me your wallet!" Again the driver quietly responded, "Charlie won't like that."

Just then the wannabe thief felt hot breath behind his neck and started to hear a low, rumbling growl. He glanced around toward the back seat. To his horror, he discovered that he was face to face with a large black panther, the man's pet. Frantic, he begged the driver, "Let me outta here!" The driver slowed down, the boy bailed out while the car was still moving, and then he ran for his life away from the road. The last glimpse of him that the amused man caught was his animated backside as he disappeared over a hill.

The teenage boy had a knife, but the driver had a Charlie. Similarly, the Canaanite king of Arad had an army, but the Israelites had something—or rather, Someone—that he hadn't counted on: the Lord.

When the Israelites left Mount Sinai and first approached Canaan from Kadesh, they could have taken the Promised Land from the south if they had cooperated with the Lord. Because of their lack of trust in Him, they lost that opportunity (Num. 14). Almost 40 years later, entering from the south was no longer a good option, apparently because the political situation there had changed. So they had to take a much longer route in order to invade Canaan from the east, across the Jordan River.

One obstacle in the path of the Israelites was the kingdom of Edom. The Israelites were relatives of the Edomites, who were descended from Esau, the twin brother of Jacob/Israel (Gen. 25; 36). So Moses appealed to the king of Edom to allow the Israelites to pass through his territory. Lacking any brotherly hospitality, he backed up his refusal with a show of force (Num. 20:14-21). The Israelites simply turned away from the confrontation rather than attacking Edom. God told Moses that He had given the Edomites their territory, so the Israelites were not to provoke them or seize any of their land (Deut. 2:5).

It was a different story when the king of Arad attacked the Israelites during their journey and captured and held some of them as prisoners. He and his people were Canaanites, not relatives of Israel, but belonging to the people whom the Israelites were to dispossess in order to take over the land of Canaan (Ex. 34:11-16). It was the king's last mistake.

"So Israel made a vow to the Lord, and said, 'If You will indeed deliver this people into my hand, then I will utterly destroy their cities.' And the Lord listened to the voice of Israel and delivered up the Canaanites, and they utterly destroyed them and their cities. So the name of that place was called Hormah" (Num. 21:2, 3; cf. the Amalekites in Exodus 17, with similar punishment in 1 Samuel 15).

After all the failures that the Israelites had experienced, including defeat by Amalekites and Canaanites as far as Hormah when the people tried to storm Canaan without God (Num. 14:45), here was an important victory of faith. It gave hope to the younger generation that they could take the Promised Land!

The name "Hormah" is from the same Hebrew root as the

verb translated "utterly destroy." This root refers to complete and irrevocable dedication of persons and/or things to the Lord, which can mean that they belong to the sanctuary or they are totally destroyed (cf. Lev. 27:21, 28, 29; Deut. 2:34; 3:6; 7:2, etc.). The nature of such dedication explains why Achan later got in trouble: He committed sacrilege by taking objects from Jericho that had been devoted to the Lord for the purpose of destruction, so he shared their destruction (Joshua 7).

Without question at certain times and places ancient Israel carried out "holy war." According to the Bible, the living God, residing with Israel, commanded or gave permission for such total destruction. He limited it to certain enemies of Israel, who would have destroyed His people if they could have, and whose iniquity was complete (cf. Gen. 15:16). The Lord could have annihilated them with fire as He did the people of Sodom and Gomorrah (Gen. 19) and as He will destroy the wicked in the end (Rev. 20). But He chose to use the Israelites as His instrument in order to test them and teach them to trust Him (cf. Judges 3:1-4).

Biblical holy war is similar in some ways to "jihad" (including the so-called terrorism that the West is fighting), which also involves total destruction that people belonging to a religious group carry out to the extent of their ability because they believe that their deity has sanctioned it. However, we find a crucial difference: Jihad against all "infidels," everywhere, has no limitations of time and space. By contrast, the God of the Bible personally controlled holy war, without making it a biblical command, and He limited it to Palestine in the period when the nation of Israel was taking its territory and becoming established there. Since the Shekinah presence of God no longer dwells on earth, and Christianity is a church rather than a nation, there can never be such a thing as legitimate Christian holy war in a literal military sense.

Look and Live

The Israelites had to take a detour around Edom because they could not pass through it (cf. Num. 20:18-21), greatly prolonging the journey to the eastern border of Canaan.

The people became impatient and raised their usual refrain that

110

God and Moses had brought them from Egypt to die in the wilderness, which had no food or water. They added their disgust for the manna that the Lord provided every day: "and we have come to loathe this miserable food" (Num. 21:5, Tanakh; cf. Num. 11:6).

At Taberah the Lord had sent fire to warn complainers (Num. 11:1). Now He sent "fiery serpents" to punish the people, and many of those bitten now perished. "Fiery" likely describes the fiery pain caused by their venom. As at Taberah, the terrified Israelites begged Moses to pray for them, which he did (Num. 21:6, 7; cf. Num. 11:2).

During the incident at Taberah God had immediately quenched the fire for the benefit of everyone (Num. 11:2), but this time He made the remedy conditional upon individual faith. "Then the Lord said to Moses, 'Make a fiery serpent, and set it on a pole; and it shall be that everyone who is bitten, when he looks at it, shall live.' So Moses made a bronze serpent, and put it on a pole; and so it was, if a serpent had bitten anyone, when he looked at the bronze serpent, he lived" (Num. 21:8, 9).

Only "when he looked" would a person recover. If someone who had been bitten refused to believe in the power of God revealed through the work of His servant Moses, he or she was perfectly free to say: "No way am I going to give in to that kind of stupidity and pretend that I may be healed if I simply look at a piece of bronze!" No problem. You can simply go on suffering and then die. The choice is yours. But if you change your mind before it is too late, just take a look. Talk about a powerful incentive at least to give faith a chance!

The metal snake had no magical power in it (although later people mistakenly worshipped it [2 Kings 18:4]). Looking at it resulted in healing from snakebite only because God made the miracle dependent on that action, just as He made the healing of Naaman's skin disease conditional on dipping seven times in the Jordan River (2 Kings 5). Performing such actions to be healed would be stupid (and indeed, Naaman thought so! [verses 11, 12]) to a person who did not believe God's word alone.

But why did Moses make a sculpture of a snake, the creature that was biting the Israelites? For one thing, they would face their problem head-on by looking at a representation of it. The Israelites had brought the snakes upon themselves by rejecting the Lord, their protector. If He had not guarded them for years along the way, they could have been bitten by snakes or stung by scorpions on any number of occasions (Deut. 8:15).

The significance of the bronze serpent has even more to it. One night Jesus explained to Nicodemus: "No one has ascended to heaven but He who came down from heaven, that is, the Son of Man who is in heaven. And as Moses lifted up the serpent in the wilderness, even so must the Son of Man be lifted up, that whoever believes in Him should not perish but have eternal life. For God so loved the world that He gave His only begotten Son, that whoever believes in Him should not perish but have everlasting life" (John 3:13-16).

Like the Israelites in the wilderness, we are all bitten and dying, but if we only choose to believe, we can live. However, Jesus was talking about eternal death and life, and He is in place of the bronze snake.

Jesus said that He must be "lifted up" as Moses raised the bronze serpent, a prophecy fulfilled when the Romans strung Him up on a cross of wood, made of a tree. In Israelite law those put to death by hanging on a tree, so that they were suspended between heaven and earth, were considered as "accursed of God" (Deut. 21:22, 23). You might think the apostles would avoid the implication that Christ was cursed. Instead, Paul rams the point home: "Christ has redeemed us from the curse of the law, having become a curse for us (for it is written, 'Cursed is everyone who hangs on a tree')" (Gal. 3:13).

But why should a snake represent Christ? Doesn't it depict sin and death, because Satan used such a creature to deceive Eve (Gen. 3)? Precisely. For God "made Him who knew no sin to be sin for us, that we might become the righteousness of God in Him" (2 Cor. 5:21).

"Imagine that! In a sense, Christ *became* sin! He bore every evil passion and selfish degradation of the billions of people who have ever inhabited our planet. With that overwhelming deluge of misery collected upon Him and identified with Him as if He were the personification of all evil, He gave Himself up for destruction in order to wipe out all sin and all of its consequences."[2]

God's remedy for snakebite and the more serious problem of

faithlessness must have been successful because the Israelites moved on to a string of victories. The first involved believing that the Lord would give them water, and cooperating with Him by digging a well at Beer (pronounced Be-er), which means "well" (Num. 21:16-18). Faith, cooperation, and water. How refreshing was that!

The next victories were major triumphs over Sihon, king of the Amorites, and Og, king of Bashan, whose realms were east of the Jordan River (verses 21-35). Both rulers attacked the Israelites, who defeated their armies in spite of the fact that the Canaanite forces were strong and Og was a giant (Deut. 3:11). Then the Israelites took and held the territories. Now the Lord's people had a base from which to strike across the Jordan into the Promised Land. At long last they were on a roll!

<hr>

[1] Max Lucado, *When God Whispers Your Name* (Dallas: Word, 1994), p. 52.
[2] Roy Gane, *Altar Call* (Berrien Springs, Mich.: Diadem, 1999), p. 77.

Chapter 10

WEAPON OF MASS DESTRUCTION

(Numbers 22-24)

Mesopotamian Maledictorian

It is disconcerting when you intend to say one thing, but something else comes out.

One time a young woman was to preach in a Spanish-speaking church. After the pastor warmly introduced her, she got up to speak. She wanted to respond by saying: "I'm embarrassed, and it's the pastor's fault!" But she used the Spanish word "embarazada," so her exclamation surprisingly came out: "I'm pregnant, and it's the pastor's fault!"

Balaam had trouble with his speech too, but it did not thwart him from saying something positive because of language translation difficulties. Rather, God prevented him from expressing something negative because He took control of him. Balaam's story (Num. 22-24) is one of the most bizarre episodes in the entire Bible.

Scripture does not tell us much about Balaam's background, but at one time he was a prophet of the true God. He apparently came from upper Mesopotamia (Num. 22:5; cf. Num. 23:7; Deut. 23:4; northeastern Syria today), where Abraham and his extended family lived for a time after they left Ur in southern Mesopotamia (Gen. 11:31). Relatives of Abraham stayed there (Gen. 24; 25; 28; 29; 31), and perhaps Balaam knew the Lord through contact with them.

As a result he seems to have been a basically good man and minister of God until he gave in to greed. His fame as a person in touch with divine power reached King Balak of Moab, who was afraid when he saw what the Israelites had done to the kings Sihon and Og (cf. Num. 21).

The Israelites were related to the Moabites, who were descended from Lot, the nephew of Abraham (Gen. 12; 19). So the Lord told the Israelites not to harrass the Moabites or take their land, just as He had commanded regarding the Edomites (Deut. 2:4-9). Thus God mercifully and patiently treated the Moabites as relatives of His people, in spite of the fact that they had turned away from Him into idolatry. But Balak, like the king of Edom, viewed Israel only as a dangerous enemy.

Assuming that Moab was the next victim, already targeted in the Israelite crosshairs, Balak was terrified. In the ancient Near East conquered kings generally had short life expectancies. To save himself and his nation, Balak decided to mount a preemptive strike. Attacking the Israelites with conventional warfare was hopeless because they had already defeated Sihon, who had been stronger than Moab (Num. 21:26-29). But Balak would deploy a "weapon of mass destruction": Balaam, whom he would hire to curse Israel. Other individuals could utter maledictions, but Balaam would do the job best.

Today we think of a curse as something that a ballplayer utters when he misses or a construction worker yells when he lands a hammer on a fingernail instead of a metal nail. We regard it as "bad language" or, in some cases, "taking God's name in vain" (breaking the third commandment [Ex. 20:7]). However, Balak did not think of a curse that way, as if Balaam would yell a bunch of unprintable four-letter anti-Semitic slogans. Such a venting of wrath and disdain could express Balak's sentiments and momentarily make him feel better, but it would not solve anything. Rather, the Moabite king viewed a curse as a real weapon because it would harness supernatural power and direct it at his enemies in a way that would actually damage them (compare curses in biblical law: Exodus 22:28; Leviticus 19:14; 24:14-16; Numbers 5:18-27).

Distinguished leaders of Moab and of Midian, an ally of Moab, came to Balaam with a handsome fee and the request of King Balak. The message did not name Israel, but referred to a certain people

115

who had come from Egypt. Balak expressed confidence that a curse by Balaam could soften up the enemy, "for I know that he whom you bless is blessed, and he whom you curse is cursed" (Num. 22:6).

The opportunity was highly attractive. Aside from the confidence shown by a faraway monarch and the chance to help a whole nation out of its distress, there was that fee . . .

That night God instructed Balaam regarding Balak's messengers: "You shall not go with them; you shall not curse the people, for they are blessed" (verse 12). Indeed, the Lord had promised Abraham: "I will make you a great nation; I will bless you and make your name great; and you shall be a blessing. I will bless those who bless you, and I will curse him who curses you; and in you all the families of the earth shall be blessed" (Gen. 12:2, 3). Later, after Abraham obeyed God's voice by almost sacrificing his son Isaac, the Lord confirmed the blessing on the patriarch and his descendants through an oath sworn by Himself (Gen. 22:15-18). A blessing does not get more permanent than that!

Even if Balaam had not been following the international news and did not identify Balak's enemy as Israel, and even if he did not know about the Lord's blessing on Abraham's descendants, the Lord's brief message was enough to settle the matter for the prophet. So he reported God's refusal to Balak's messengers and sent them home (Num. 22:13). That should have been the end of the Balaam story.

Desperate, Balak did not take no for an answer. So he sent an even weightier delegation to Balaam, with an offer that was a blank check for him to fill in whatever amount he chose: "For I will certainly honor you greatly, and I will do whatever you say to me" (verse 17). Nevertheless, Balaam replied: "Though Balak were to give me his house full of silver and gold, I could not go beyond the word of the Lord my God, to do less or more" (verse 18). This sounds like a man of integrity and strong principles!

Balaam already had his answer from God and should have immediately sent Balak's emissaries back to Moab. But he invited them to stay the night in case the Lord should have anything more to say, betraying his hope that God would change His mind to permit him to take advantage of the most profitable commission of his prophetic career.

To Balaam's delight, God did tell him, "If the men come to call you, rise and go with them; but only the word which I speak to you—that you shall do" (verse 20). Notice the word "if." Balaam was to go only if the messengers of Balak called on him in the morning. That was the sign. But they didn't. So he had no right to go. Nevertheless, he ignored the "if," saddled his female donkey, and took off after the Moabite princes. Thus he disobeyed the Lord, flunking the divine test of his character.

Balaam journeyed with his two servants, not with the Moabites, apparently because he had not yet caught up with them. He was in a hurry to make up for lost time and did not want to lose his grand opportunity. So he undoubtedly urged his donkey to go as fast as she could.

God was angry with Balaam, so the "Angel of the Lord" blocked his way as an adversary or accuser (verse 22). Here the Hebrew word for "adversary" is *satan,* referring to antagonistic function. The text does not use it as the proper name Satan—that is, the devil. Elsewhere in the Bible the angel or messenger of the Lord who appears to human beings can be the Lord Himself (for example, Judges 6; 13). When this is so, the angel must be Christ (Judges 13:18—His name is "Wonderful" [cf. Isa. 9:6]), because He is the member of the divine Trinity who has entered human history (Micah 5:2) to communicate with human beings (John 1—"the Word"). So it is possible that Balaam encountered Christ, the divine guardian of Israel.

In any case, the powerful supernatural being standing in the road to meet Balaam held a drawn sword and was ready to use it on the prophet who had enthusiastically set out to speak in God's name without His permission. The Lord is hard on false prophets and ministers who do that, because they hurt people by speaking falsely in His name, thereby taking His name in vain (cf. Ex. 20:7). Such people are dangerous because they commit "identity theft" against God Himself, using His name and authority to make whole groups of people believe things they would not otherwise. The Lord holds them seriously accountable. For example: "Then the prophet

117

Jeremiah said to Hananiah the prophet, 'Hear now, Hananiah, the Lord has not sent you, but you make this people trust in a lie. Therefore thus says the Lord: "Behold, I will cast you from the face of the earth. This year you shall die, because you have taught rebellion against the Lord."' So Hananiah the prophet died the same year in the seventh month" (Jer. 28:15–17).

Balaam, who was supposed to be a prophet of the Lord and therefore a "seer," meaning one who sees what others cannot (cf. 1 Sam. 9:9), was rushing headlong to his death because he did not see the angel of the Lord. His lowly donkey, however, sensed the being and tried to evade harm three times. Because Balaam was not about to let the Moabites get away from him, he beat his animal to force it to continue.

Just when the prophet's anger had risen to the point that he was hitting his donkey unmercifully with his stick, she asked him why he had struck her. Rather than stopping to think about the fact that he was having a conversation with a donkey, Balaam replied: "Because you have abused me. I wish there were a sword in my hand, for now I would kill you!" (Num. 22:29). Oh really! Someone waited nearby with a sword, and He would be the judge of who was doing the abusing.

Against Balaam's accusation that the animal was playing a dirty trick on him, the donkey responded: "'Am I not your donkey on which you have ridden, ever since I became yours, to this day? Was I ever disposed to do this to you?' And he said, 'No'" (verse 30). Thus the mighty, brilliant Balaam, who was hiring himself out to destroy an entire nation with a curse from his lips, had lost an argument with a donkey! She could see the supernatural, like a prophet. He could not. The animal had spoken the truth, which the Lord had put in its mouth. He had not. The donkey had reacted intelligently and logically. Balaam had responded stubbornly . . . like . . . a donkey! We expect him to start braying any minute.

The biting, sarcastic irony of this story, in which Balaam and his donkey reverse roles, is outrageously hilarious. It also sends a powerful message to those who foolishly presume to put themselves on a collision course with God by seeking to harm His people for any reason (cf. Esther 6, in which Haman makes a fool of himself when he and Mordecai reverse roles). The Lord has placed the blessing of His name/identity on them (cf. Num. 6:22-27), so anyone who tries to curse or attack them is assaulting God.

When the Lord opened Balaam's eyes and he saw the angel, he fell flat on his face. The angel of the Lord rebuked him for striking his donkey and made it clear that the creature had saved his life (Num. 22:31-33). By mistreating her, Balaam had betrayed the evil side of his character. "A righteous man regards the life of his animal, but the tender mercies of the wicked are cruel" (Prov. 12:10). Life is sacred, and those who cherish and nurture animal life will likely do the same for human life. Conversely, those who have no qualms about hurting animals tend to inflict suffering on other people more easily. Balaam beat his donkey because she interfered with his greed, and neither did he care about thousands of Israelites.

Balaam's donkey protested: "Am I not your donkey on which you have ridden, ever since I became yours, to this day? Was I ever disposed to do this to you?" Perhaps the principle of this miraculous speech could apply to the way people treat each other: "Am I not your spouse/employee with which you have lived/worked, ever since I became yours, to this day? Was I ever disposed to do this to you?" Rather than treating our faithful helpers badly because we think they have messed up, how about giving them the benefit of the doubt? Perhaps they have reasons for their actions that so far we have missed. If we listen, we might learn something!

Now that he was caught, Balaam readily confessed to the angel, "I have sinned, for I did not know You stood in the way against me. Now therefore, if it displeases You, I will turn back" (Num. 22:34). "If it displeases You!" Is there any question? What do you mean "if"? Balaam should have simply turned around and gone back home. But in spite of his near brush with death, he really did want to go to Moab.

Surprisingly, the angel of the Lord allowed Balaam to continue on and do what he wanted, but insisted: "Only the word that I speak to you, that you shall speak" (verse 35; cf. verse 20). Getting what he wanted was not good for greedy Balaam, just as heaps of quail were not good for the Israelites at Kibroth Hattaavah (Num. 11). God allowed them to proceed in order to teach (if possible) and test them, not because His will was weak. In the process the Lord could overrule Balaam's curses and reveal to whole nations what the blessing on His people meant.

Unexpected Blessings

When Balaam met his client, Balak, he protected himself from the possibility of failure to meet the king's lofty expectations by expressing a disclaimer, which served like an escape clause in a contract: "Have I any power at all to say anything? The word that God puts in my mouth, that I must speak" (Num. 22:38). It would be a bit like a doctor saying to a patient, "We'll do the best we can, but there are factors that we can't control, so we can't guarantee the results."

Balaam should have said: "God has blessed the Israelites and forbids me to curse them, so we are wasting our time and your money!" What was he thinking? That God would change His mind? Or that Balak would be satisfied with something other than a curse that really could damage Israel? Shackled by the shimmer of shekels, Balaam was getting entangled in a lose–lose situation. He was like a gambler in Las Vegas when there is no money in the jackpot, or a Russian roulette player when all six spinning chambers of the pistol pointed at his head are loaded. Greed has a way of making a person dangerously illogical!

The prophet received and apparently partook of Balak's pagan Moabite sacrifices, and the next day the king took him up to a pagan place called "Bamoth-baal," meaning "the high places of (the god) Baal" (verses 40, 41). Balaam was compromising his principles by conforming to the ways of unbelievers through participating in their religious practices. Fitting in like this is the diplomatic, "nice," and politically correct thing to do. It is also the slippery slope to certain apostasy.

Interestingly, archaeologists have found an ancient group of inscriptions that tell about Balaam. They date to the eighth century B.C. (during the time of the Israelite monarchy), and were found on plaster walls at the site of Deir 'Allā , just east of the Jordan River.

The texts remember Balaam as a prophet of the gods, who communicate an alarming message to him in a night vision. The account portrays him as participating in polytheistic, pagan religion and divination. The similarities to the biblical account are striking.

Bamoth-baal was a high location from which Balaam could view the edge of the Israelite encampment (verse 41). By "line of sight" he could aim his curses at their target! In order to invoke the Lord favorably, Balaam had Balak offer an expensive group of sacrifices. Sure enough, God gave Balaam a message to speak in the presence of the Moabite king and his princes. The Lord was playing along with Balaam's game in order to achieve His own purpose!

He was working all things together for good for His chosen people (see Rom. 8:28). Balaam's first inspired speech recounted Balak's request to curse Israel and continued:

"How shall I curse whom God has not cursed? And how shall I denounce whom the Lord has not denounced?" (Num. 23:8). The prophet went on to observe that Israel was special and its people numerous. He ended: "Let me die the death of the righteous, and let my end be like his!" (verse 10), thus identifying himself with righteous Israel!

King Balak was upset, but Balaam simply cited his escape clause: He could utter only speech that the Lord gave him. Balak understood what that meant, but he was desperate and refused to give up. Perhaps another location, where the prophet would see less of the Israelite encampment and not be as impressed, would work better. So he took Balaam to a mountain peak (Pisgah) and wasted more valuable animals as sacrifices.

Balak had the pagan notion that he could manipulate the deity by doing things in different places. But that wouldn't change anything. It reminds me of the time my wife and I were trying to enjoy a peaceful Sabbath afternoon walk in a northern California forest. Our baby daughter was in a pack on my back, but for some reason she didn't want to be there on that particular occasion, and kept crying loudly. I turned to my wife and plaintively suggested: "Let's get out of here and go to a quiet place!"

We cannot manipulate or outwit God. He sees and owns

everything, everywhere. So token gifts, which He does not need for Himself anyway, cannot induce Him to overlook violations of His will by hypocrites (Ps. 50:16-23). The Moabite king wanted to slander his relatives, the Israelites, and he supposed that the Lord was like him (cf. Ps. 50:21—"You thought that I was altogether like you"). But the true path of salvation was to repent and accept the lordship of the true God.

Balaam uttered words from the Lord a second time. The first time had been a brief warning. Having disregarded that, Balak now received a major dose. The prophet started by affirming that God's blessing is unalterable because He is not like a changeable human being (Num. 23:19, 20). The next words were surprising: "He has not observed iniquity in Jacob, nor has He seen wickedness in Israel. The Lord his God is with him, and the shout of a King is among them" (verse 21). What about all those terrible rebellions by the Israelites? Had the Lord forgotten about them? In a sense, yes, because He had forgiven His people as a nation. They were not perfect, but they belonged to Him, and He was with them. He may discipline His people, but He doesn't air their dirty laundry before outsiders. Similarly, the Lord's people should settle their problems and disputes among themselves as much as possible to avoid defaming the reputation of their community, and therefore that of God in the world (cf. 1 Cor. 6).

To Balak, it was ominous that "the shout of a King is among them." The 12 tribes were not a bunch of disorganized, scruffy hoodlums, a "dirty dozen" with more arrogance than readiness to "rumble." They were a powerful royal army, with central coordination by a great ruler. Their king was the divine Lord Himself, who had brought them out of Egypt! Therefore, no sorcery or divination could withstand Israel, which was as strong as an ox and as deadly as a lion (Num. 23:22-24). The divine warning was powerful. As the psalmist said: "Now consider this, you who forget God, lest I tear you in pieces, and there be none to deliver" (Ps. 50:22).

Alarmed, Balak got the point and ordered Balaam neither to curse nor bless Israel. In other words: "Just shut up before you do any more damage!" Again Balaam reminded the king of his escape clause. But

Balak wanted to give Balaam three strikes before he was out. Maybe yet another place would work: the summit of Peor, overlooking the wasteland. So more animals died for nothing (Num. 23:25-30).

Balaam saw his opportunity for enjoying the lifestyle of the rich and famous slipping away. So this time he did not try to meet the Lord in order to receive a message from Him, but sought to short-circuit the divine connection that restrained his speech. Perhaps he could get away with uttering a curse, even if the Lord was not behind it, in order to make Balak think he was doing the job for which he had been hired. However, the Spirit of God had no trouble finding him and controlling him (Num. 24:1, 2), just as the Spirit had come upon Eldad and Medad, who prophesied even though they were away from the sanctuary (Num. 11:26).

Looking down upon the orderly array of unsuspecting Israelites, Balaam uttered a prophetic oracle that first identified him as "the man whose eyes are opened, . . . him who hears the words of God, who sees the vision of the Almighty, who falls down, with eyes wide open" (Num. 24:3, 4; see also verses 15, 16). It seems to be a reminder of the way he saw and heard the angel of the Lord and fell prostrate before Him (Num. 22:31-35). Submitted to God like that, Balaam would speak the truth. Oh, that he would live up to these words when the Spirit of the Lord was not overriding his will (cf. 1 Sam. 19:20-24 and the case of King Saul)!

Balaam went on to praise the Israelite encampment and King, to repeat that the Lord had brought His people out of Egypt, and to warn that they were strong enough to crush their enemies (Num. 24:5-8). He concluded by echoing the Lord's promise to Abraham: "Blessed is he who blesses you, and cursed is he who curses you" (verse 9; cf. Gen. 12:3).

Furious, Balak told Balaam to get lost! The Lord had kept Balaam from honor. But again the prophet reminded the king of his escape clause. Yes, he was going home, but first he would give Balak another oracle for free. The king had been warned that it was dangerous to mess with Israel. Now Balaam would explicitly prophesy what the Israelites would do to the Moabites (and other peoples) later on (Num. 24:10-25).

Predictions of the Distant Future

Under divine inspiration, Balaam again identified himself as the man whose eyes are opened, etc. But this time his prophetic sight penetrated centuries into the future with startling accuracy: "I see Him, but not now; I behold Him, but not near; a Star shall come out of Jacob; a Scepter shall rise out of Israel, and batter the brow of Moab, and destroy all the sons of tumult. And Edom shall be a possession; Seir also, his enemies, shall be a possession, while Israel does valiantly. Out of Jacob One shall have dominion, and destroy the remains of the city" (verses 17-19).

As Balaam predicted, King David conquered Moab and Edom (2 Sam. 8). A millennium later, another royal "Star" appeared. In fact, a star signaled His birth (Matt. 2). In the ancient world a star could represent divinity. For example, the early Sumerian (southern Mesopotamian, before Abraham) sign for "god" had the shape of a star. So the star of Bethlehem fittingly announced the entrance of the Son of God into the human race.

David was a gloriously successful conqueror and ruler for a few decades. But Christ, the divine Son of David, "will reign over the house of Jacob forever, and of His kingdom there will be no end" (Luke 1:33). He will triumph over not only a portion of the Near East, but the entire world (Rev. 19:11-21).

It is astounding that God gave Balaam such a breathtaking prophecy, which must have left King Balak and the Moabite princes speechless. Obviously the Lord was mercifully reaching out to Gentile nations through Balaam, in spite of his motivation and character. If he, the Moabites, and their Midianite allies could learn to respect Israel and its God, they and others within their sphere of influence would have the opportunity to accept His lordship and receive His blessings.

Since the Lord could use Balaam, with all his faults, perhaps He can employ other unlikely people of our modern world to carry out His purposes and pave the way for them to receive the full gospel of Christ. Should this happen, God's people would do well to look at the big picture and take advantage of opportunities rather than focusing on details to condemn and criticize when things aren't done exactly our way.

For example, when Mel Gibson produced *The Passion of the Christ,* the fact that the movie was too violent, too mystical, or not completely accurate to the Bible offended some Christians. But this shocking, unsanitized portrayal profoundly moved people, including many nonbelievers, to think about what Jesus went through in terms of characteristically nasty Roman torture and execution, not adequately including the unfilmable "second death" separation from His Father! It gave them an opportunity to think about and choose salvation from the dominion of Satan. Talking to anyone about Christ was easy and natural after the film appeared. I had such conversations with the person who cuts my hair and the mechanic who changes the oil in my car.

Balaam finished up his speech by pronouncing doom on various nations (including enemies of Israel) that were unblessed by contrast with Israel. Then he went home (Num. 24:20-25). His bid for glory and riches had failed. Balak's plan to save Moab had not only collapsed—it had backfired: Israel was blessed, and Moab was cursed. Now Balak would need to find a way for his country to survive as a nonprophet organization.

When he and Balaam went their separate ways, it looked like the end of their story.

Unfortunately for Israel and for them, it wasn't (see Num. 25; 31).

Chapter 11

WEAPONS OF MASS DISTRACTION

(Numbers 25)

Food and Sex

When you are poised for a D-day invasion, it is wise to be focused and prepare for what you are about to do. The Israelites paused on the east side of the Jordan River, about to cross it and invade their Promised Land. Rather than getting ready, however, they lost their focus and nearly aborted their mission because they became too chummy with apparently harmless civilians who were actually deadly enemies.

The Israelites were camped at Shittim ("acacia trees") when some Moabite girls started showing up to invite Israelites to feasts. How hospitable of them to share with travelers! The food was a welcome nonvegetarian change from the usual manna, and the parties with those attractive visitors were lots of fun.

Oh, a couple of details: The food was from sacrifices to Moabite gods. To be polite, the Israelites not only enjoyed eating it, but also bowed down to idols of the various gods. It was obviously the thing to do. Surely it couldn't do any harm. But what made idolatrous worship really desirable was the fact that the worship liturgy included sex with those seductive girls. Food and sex—ever the ways to a man's heart! God created legitimate desires for both things, but sin hijacks them to lead away from God.

Numbers 25:1 reports that the Israelites began to be promiscuous with Moabite women.

Obviously it refers to indulging their sexual lust. But in the process they were also spiritually adulterous. They bonded themselves to the local god—Baal of Peor—and thereby violated their exclusive, intimate covenant relationship with the Lord (verse 3) by breaking the first of the Ten Commandments: "You shall have no other gods before Me" (Ex. 20:3).

The Israelites were leaving the wilderness and coming in contact with idolatrous peoples, who could easily corrupt them. Their interaction with the local inhabitants would continually challenge their faithfulness to God. Their first test had arrived, and they had already flunked it. Just after the golden calf apostasy, the Lord had warned the Israelites of this very danger: "You shall not make a covenant with the inhabitants of the land, for when they prostitute themselves to their gods and sacrifice to their gods, someone among them will invite you, and you will eat of the sacrifice" (Ex. 34:15, NRSV). Later the Lord assured the Israelites that they would have more trouble with idolatry in the future: After the death of Moses, "this people will begin to prostitute themselves to the foreign gods in their midst, the gods of the land into which they are going; they will forsake me, breaking my covenant that I have made with them" (Deut 31:16, NRSV).

The rebellion led by the unfaithful scouts had led God to instruct the Israelites to put tassels, including a bluish (or violet-colored) cord, on the hems of their garments (Num. 15:37-40). He explained that it would help them to maintain their holy connection with Him by remembering and doing all of His commandments instead of following the temptations of their eyes and hearts (verse 39, NRSV). They had a strong tendency to put their own hearts and eyes, representing their minds, emotions, and senses, in place of God. Things that were attractive to them were deadly dangerous, as the fruit of a certain tree was to Eve. God's people could be safe only if they followed divine guidance by faith.

Nothing has changed! With all our increased education and knowledge, and with the explosion of sensory temptations coming at us through various media, we are in no less danger of following our minds and hearts rather than the Lord and His revealed will. It is easy to make up our minds first and then rationalize away any indications of God's Word to the contrary. After all, we are so much more enlightened than those old prophets speaking to their primitive culture. Nobody living in another century, even a recent one, could possibly understand and adequately speak to our situation. Old blueprints are simply obsolete.

No! The wise man has rightly said: "That which has been is what will be, that which is done is what will be done, and there is nothing new under the sun" (Eccl. 1:9). This is not to advocate a circular view of history, but to recognize that people are people. So advancements in knowledge and technology do not alter basic human nature. Specifics may change, but we have the same categories of temptations and responses. It is why Christ could be "in all points tempted as we are" (Heb. 4:15), even though He lived two millennia ago during the time of the Roman Empire, before cigarettes, automobiles, and the Internet. The fact that we still possess the same traits explains how the Bible can be a timeless revelation of divine principles that are just as applicable to us as they were to people in bygone eras. To ignore, bypass, or underemphasize them is shortsighted, arrogant, and just plain stupid.

Needless to say, when Israel "got in bed" with the Baal of Peor, it aroused the righteous anger of the divine husband (Num. 25:3). Anyone who wonders why God was upset should ask the question: How would I feel if I came home and found my spouse in bed with somebody else? "For jealousy is a husband's fury; therefore he will not spare in the day of vengeance. He will accept no recompense" (Prov. 6:34, 35). Such "jealousy" is not petty envy—it is rightful, zealous protection of exclusive intimacy to which both parties have agreed in a solemn, permanent covenant of love. "Set me as a seal upon your heart, as a seal upon your arm; for love is as strong as death, jealousy as cruel as the grave; its flames are flames of fire, a most vehement flame. Many waters cannot quench love, nor can the floods drown it. If a man would give for love all the wealth of his house, it would be utterly despised" (Song of Sol. 8:6, 7).

Holding Leaders Accountable

Anyone who listens to the news or picks up a history book realizes that politically or economically powerful people often regard themselves as above the law and believe that they can get away with murder. It was like that in ancient Mesopotamia during the time of the patriarchs: The law code of Hammurabi allowed lighter penalties if a higher-status citizen killed a lesser person than it did if the murderer belonged to a lower class than the victim.

Israelite law leveled the playing field with what we could term "equal opportunity punishment" in the area of criminal jurisprudence (Lev. 24:17, 19-22; Num. 35:31). Under religious law, a leader/chieftain bore extra responsibility before God when he sinned, as shown by the fact that he had to bring a separate sin offering (Lev. 4:22-26—male goat). The greatest responsibility for sin lay on the high priest, who exerted the most religious influence. His sin offering was equivalent to that required of the entire community (verses 3-12, 13-21).

When Israelite leaders made mistakes that harmed the Lord's reputation or led their people astray, God held them accountable for their influence. Thus Nadab and Abihu were "fired" from being priests (Lev. 10), Miriam was smitten with skin disease (Num. 12), Korah and his fellow leaders were buried alive or burned up (Num. 16), and Moses and Aaron were barred from the Promised Land (Num. 20). So the Lord's response to apostasy at Shittim by the Jordan River is not so surprising. He told Moses: " 'Take all the leaders of the people and hang the offenders before the Lord, out in the sun, that the fierce anger of the Lord may turn away from Israel.' So Moses said to the judges of Israel, 'Every one of you kill his men who were joined to Baal of Peor' " (Num. 25:4, 5).

Moses' made it clear that the Israelites were to execute their tribal leaders (literally "heads of the people") because they had led the way into apostasy.

Compare what happened after the people worshiped the golden calf: The men of the tribe of Levi, who chose to be on the Lord's side, had executed unfaithful fellow Israelites (Ex. 32:26-28).

God's covenant people were always to root out any idolatry that appeared among them, without sparing or pitying their kinsmen (Deut. 13). While it may appear harsh, idolatry broke the covenant with God that made it possible for the nation to survive. Any

129

Israelite who turned to other gods or even quietly advocated such an approach jeopardized the entire people. Therefore, the other Israelites had to stop such individuals in their tracks, as if they were an Osama bin Laden brandishing a weapon of mass destruction in New York City. Any Israelite practicing idolatry knew better and could be only an archenemy of God. So when he or she was caught, it was time for an execution, not a Bible study.

Today God's people belong to a church, not a state. So we obviously should never think of trying to execute or even dismember the members of our spiritual community who go astray and attempt to take others with them. But the Lord's reputation and the integrity of His people and their mission still matters. Nobody should ever be allowed to derail us from following God or lead us into conveniently assimilating with other "faiths" that are marching to the beats of different drummers.

We should follow due process (Matt. 18:15-20) in holding accountable—to the point of cutting ties with, if necessary—anyone who tries to turn us from our loyalty to the Lord and His gospel mission outreach for our time (see especially Matt. 28:19, 20; Rev. 14:6-12). Pastors, teachers, and administrators are more accountable, in proportion to their influence. They do not own the church—they only work there. The church belongs to God, and He will run it His way.

The Lord said to Moses, "Hang the offenders before the Lord, out in the sun, that the fierce anger of the Lord may turn away from Israel" (Num. 25:4). The word for "hang" does not mean "strangle on a noose," but "string up" or "impale." Displaying a dead body like this in full view ("out in the sun"), as the Italians did to the dictator Mussolini and his mistress near the end of World War II, is not a pretty sight and makes a major statement. Compare the way the Philistines displayed the decapitated body of their enemy, King Saul, by fastening it to the wall of Beth Shan, along with the bodies of his sons (1 Sam. 31:10, 12).

We find still another story in which stringing bodies up before the Lord served to remove His wrath from Israel. During David's reign a terrible famine lasted three years.

An inquiry to the Lord revealed that the famine had resulted because King Saul had unjustly tried to exterminate the Gibeonites, who were protected by an oath even though they were Canaanites (2 Sam. 21:1, 2; Joshua 9). To make atonement in the sense of removing the guilt on behalf of the land and its people, Saul was punished after his death by losing some of his sons and grandsons (compare David's punishment of losing his infant son born to Bathsheba [2 Sam. 12:15-18]). It was Saul's punishment, but his household continued to bear guilt because his family members were a corporate continuation of him (cf. 1 Kings 2:31-33). After they were killed and then strung up in the open, the Lord heeded the entreaty for the land, implying that the famine then came to an end (2 Sam. 21:3-14).

The tragic stories of Shittim and of Saul have several key elements in common:

1. Leaders received punishment for massive crimes.

2. Punishment involved exposing corpses rather than immediately burying them.

3. The punishment on the offenders served as a kind of "atonement" to turn away divine anger.

These cases did not involve substitutionary atonement in the sense that Christ, who was completely innocent and from an innocent "household," died in our place. However, atonement through stringing a person up was similar to the cross event. During the 1980s I was studying the book of Numbers in an advanced Hebrew seminar at the University of California at Berkeley. Professor Jacob Milgrom, a rabbi, taught it. When we came to Numbers 25:4, he surprisingly observed that he could understand why the followers of Jesus could interpret the fact that He was strung up (on a cross) as a means of atonement.

As the sentence of the Lord through Moses was about to be carried out on the leaders, Moses and the people wept outside the tabernacle. They were mourning at the fall of these men, not rejoicing. It is always a terrible tragedy when the elect—or the elected— are deceived (cf. Matt. 24:24).

Atonement Through Execution

Rather than grieving, somebody else was in another mood.

Parading by in full view of the mourners came an Israelite man leading a Midianite woman to his relatives inside the camp (Num. 25:6). They were obviously planning to fool around with her. The man was Zimri, son of a Simeonite chieftain, and she was Cozbi, daughter of a Midianite chieftain (verses 14, 15).

Remember that the Midianites had allied with the Moabites (Num. 22:4, 7).

Zimri's flagrant, reckless lust brought the crisis of apostasy to a dramatic climax. As Zimri took Cozbi into a tent and they started getting cozy, Phinehas got up and fetched a spear.

As son of the new high priest, Eleazar (now that Aaron was dead), Phinehas had charge of the Levites guarding the sanctuary (cf. Num. 3:32). So he knew what to do with a weapon. He followed the pair into the tent and thrust the spear through both of them (Num. 25:7, 8).

At this point the biblical text reports the shocking news that meanwhile a plague from the Lord had already begun and 24,000 had died. It was the largest body count for a single occasion during the entire journey of the Israelites from Egypt to Canaan. The stakes were highest when the second generation was about to enter the Promised Land. But when Phinehas executed Zimri and Cozbi, the plague ceased (verses 8, 9). As had happened years earlier when Aaron ran among the people with incense, swift action by a priest made atonement to halt a plague and save the community (Num. 16:46-50).

Through Moses, the Lord announced a special reward for Phinehas, who had saved his people by prompt and pointed action.

"Phinehas the son of Eleazar, the son of Aaron the priest, has turned back My wrath from the children of Israel, because he was zealous with My zeal among them, so that I did not consume the children of Israel in My zeal. Therefore say, 'Behold, I give to him My covenant of peace; and it shall be to him and his descendants after him a covenant of an everlasting priesthood, because he was zealous for his God, and made atonement for the children of Israel' " (Num. 25:11-13).

Though he was already a priest, the Lord made him a covenant promise that he would inherit the high priesthood, which would then belong to his descendants (compare Judges 20:28, in which he is high priest during the early period of the judges). He had accomplished atonement for the Israelite community, not by offering a sacrifice that represented the substitutionary death of Christ, but in a more basic, nonsubstitutionary sense: by eliminating the offenders from the community. Zimri and Cozbi received no benefit from this kind of atonement.

Like Christ, Phinehas was consumed with the Lord's zeal (cf. John 2:14-17). Being zealous is not necessarily a good thing. One can be sincerely and enthusiastically misguided, as many fascists, communists, and religious fanatics have been. Some people are so zealous that they almost froth at the mouth, and you wonder if they have missed their rabies booster shot. But allowing the Lord to inspire and control zeal that is according to His principles and furthers His mission in the world is excellent, and we need a lot more of it. Today our zeal will not involve impaling people with spears, but by God's grace we can help them get the point in other ways.

The Lord had good news for Phinehas, but bad news for the Midianites: "Harass the Midianites, and attack them; for they harassed you with their schemes by which they seduced you in the matter of Peor and in the matter of Cozbi" (Num. 25:17, 18). Wait a minute! What is this about "schemes," referring to deceitfulness or trickery (compare the Hebrew verb *kzb,* "lie/deceive," which sounds similar to Cozbi)? The Moabites and Midianites must have cooperated in a conspiracy to bring trouble to the Israelites by seducing them into immorality and idolatry. What a brilliant idea—to drive a wedge between the Israelites and their God so that He would destroy them!

Who could be the mastermind to hatch up such a devilishly clever plot? Who would understand the relationship between the Lord and His people that well? Later we will get a massive hint. When the Israelites attacked the Midianites, who of all people should show up in their midst? "Balaam the son of Beor they also killed with the sword" (Num. 31:8). What was he doing there? The last that we had heard of him, he had gone home (Num. 24:25).

After failing to curse Israel, Balaam must have pondered how to get his reward another way—without interference from God. For Balak, cursing was only a potential means to an end. What he really cared about was weakening Israel down to a manageable level. So Balaam offered him and his Midianite allies another kind of weapon of mass destruction: the Lord's wrath upon Israelites who violated His covenant (Num. 31:16). All it took to lure 24,000 Israelites to speedy graves was the mass distraction of some eye-sizzling women and mouth-watering food. And now we know . . . the rest of the story.

The prophet's final success led to his destruction. He was like a large bull moose that charged a speeding train and succeeded in temporarily derailing its front wheels. But that was the end of the moose.

Balaam died long ago, but the legacy of his proven tactics lives on. The apostle Peter warns of people who "have forsaken the right way and gone astray, following the way of Balaam the son of Beor, who loved the wages of unrighteousness" (2 Peter 2:15). John records a message from Christ to the church in Pergamum, which includes the warning: "But I have a few things against you, because you have there those who hold the doctrine of Balaam, who taught Balak to put a stumbling block before the children of Israel, to eat things sacrificed to idols, and to commit sexual immorality" (Rev. 2:14).

We are just as vulnerable as the Israelites were. Dangers do not decrease as we get closer to our Promised Land. Rather, as the enemy's time grows shorter, he has greater incentive to destroy us by any means at his disposal (Rev. 12:12). He is waging a "Battle of the Bulge" and throwing "Hail Mary" shots all over the place. Our only safety is in staying with the Lord. If He is for us, "who can be against us?" (Rom. 8:31). Nothing and nobody can separate us from His love (verses 35-39).

Chapter 12

A NEW GENERATION

(Numbers 26–30)

Regroup and Move On

An army that suffers heavy casualties must regroup and move on. After the terrible plague at Shittim, the Israelites needed more organization and instructions before taking the Promised Land. The first step was a repetition of what had happened 40 years before, at the beginning of the book of Numbers. The Lord had ordered a military census of all Israelite men who were 20 years old and above (Num. 1). The total was 603,550, not including the Levites (verse 46). That army should have conquered Canaan.

The Lord demonstrated His power on behalf of the generation that left Egypt with a greater concentration of miracles than anywhere else in the Old Testament. Tragically, the people never developed personal trust in Him. When the report of 10 scouts terrified them, they refused to believe that God was capable of presenting them with the land. So He gave them their just deserts:

"The carcasses of you who have complained against Me shall fall in this wilderness, all of you who were numbered, according to your entire number, from twenty years old and above. Except for Caleb the son of Jephunneh and Joshua the son of Nun, you shall by no means enter the land which I swore I would make you dwell in" (Num. 14:29, 30).

At the end of the 40 years in the wilderness, the census process had to be redone in order to organize a new army of the younger generation. It could not include any of the older generation, except

135

for Caleb and Joshua. Sure enough, when Israel's leaders tabulated all the 601,730 men 20 years old and above, none had been counted in the earlier census except the two faithful scouts (Num. 26:64, 65). All the rest were in desert graves.

In Egypt the population of Israelites had exploded, to the consternation of Pharaoh (Ex. 1). But in the wilderness, the number of adult males decreased during the 40 years because of such factors as the plagues for rebellion against the Lord. Some tribes fared better than others. The tribe of Simeon, to which the rebel Zimri belonged (Num. 25:14), dramatically decreased from 59,300 (Num. 1:23) to 22,200 (Num. 26:14). It meant that Simeon would receive a smaller territory in Canaan, while other tribes that had been more faithful to God and maintained their numbers in the wilderness would receive larger inheritances (verses 52-56).

The census report on the tribe of Reuben reminds us that Dathan and Abiram, two Reubenite representatives, contended against Moses as part of the company of Korah (a Levite). They had died as a warning sign/example when the earth swallowed them, and fire consumed 250 men (verses 9, 10). We knew all that (see Num. 16). But now we learn something new and startling: "The sons of Korah, however, did not die" (Num. 26:11, Tanakh).

The entire families of Dathan and Abiram perished with them (Num. 16:27, 32), so their lines of descendants were instantly cut off as a divine punishment. Korah's sons (or children), on the other hand, continued. The Bible does not tell us the reason. Perhaps it was because they had already showed faithfulness to God. This possibility receives support from the book of Psalms, in which later descendants of Korah appear as the authors of some of the greatest hymns of faith and praise in the Bible.

One of their compositions is Psalm 46, which begins: "God is our refuge and strength, a very present help in trouble. Therefore we will not fear, even though the earth be removed, and though the mountains be carried into the midst of the sea" (verses 1, 2). This passage served as the inspiration for Martin Luther's famous hymn, "A Mighty Fortress Is Our God." We see hope for the future when the children of an old rebel choose to go exactly the opposite direction and loyally follow the Lord. With His amazing grace and wisdom, He knew what He was doing when He let the sons of Korah live. For thousands of years His people have been stronger because of their eloquent encouragement.

To Keep the Circle Unbroken

A person whose name becomes attached to a place is remembered centuries later. Alexandria, Colombia, and Washington, D.C., keep names of specific people alive. An individual who lacks such a memorial, or whose connection to a place gets erased, can vanish from memory. Thus many scholars did not believe that a King Sargon ruled the Neo-Assyrian empire, as Isaiah said (Isa. 20:1), until archaeologists unearthed the destroyed city called "The Fortress of Sargon," which had his name written all over it.

An Israelite by the name of Zelophehad had a problem, even though he was dead.

Normally his sons would carry on his name, which would become attached to a piece of the Promised Land that they would inherit. Zelophehad was blessed with plenty of children, all right, but they were all daughters. Israelite custom did not allow females to inherit land. Such a practice kept property intact within an extended family. Otherwise, a woman who married outside her clan would take ownership of property with her to the family of her husband and thereby diminish the holdings of her original clan. Land was crucial to each clan because it provided the means for an agricultural livelihood.

Zelophehad would have no inheritance in the Promised Land to maintain the memory of his name (Num. 27:1-4). Ancient Israelites regarded their children as continuing their lives, in a sense, by carrying on their identity. Society regarded it as so important that if a man died without children, his brother would have a child with the deceased man's wife, and everyone would regard the child as belonging to the dead man (see Gen. 38; Ruth 4). In fact, a law from the Lord upheld and regulated the custom of brother-in-law marriage (Deut. 25:5-10).

In modern Western culture we rightly apply God's principles of respect for the dead and care for widows in other ways. When dealing with biblical laws, we will get in trouble if we just read and do.

We must read and think before doing, as Paul urged Timothy to use the word of truth correctly (2 Tim. 2:15). So we do not need to practice brother-in-law marriage in our culture.

Naturally, Zelophehad's fate disturbed his daughters, who thought it was unfair. It is true that their father belonged to the generation that God had condemned to die in the wilderness, but the descendants of others who had thus perished would have property. We should not confuse the young women with modern-day feminists—they were primarily sticking up for the rights of their father.

The daughters felt confident enough to present their case before Moses and the other leaders of Israel, who gave them a respectful hearing. The leaders did not simply rule against them on the basis of past custom. Instead, they sought God's guidance. The Lord readily agreed with the practical solution proposed by the daughters of Zelophehad, namely, that their father's inheritance should pass to them, as it would if they were sons. In fact, God made their case a precedent for what should happen in the future if a man died without a son (Num. 27:4-11). In Numbers 36 He added that daughters of such a man should marry within their clan in order to keep the property within that group.

It is easy for a modern reader to underestimate the importance of this biblical passage, unless she is an African woman. Under African customary law a female cannot inherit, even from her husband. So if a wife becomes a widow, the relatives of her husband take the property that she shared with her husband, which is often her only source of livelihood. She can return to her own blood relatives, if they are willing to provide for her. In many cases, however, she has nowhere to go and faces two gruesome options: starve to death or sell her body into prostitution and risk dying of HIV (AIDS) while contributing to the spread of the disease. Change of the inheritance law, in harmony with international legal principles of nondiscrimination recognized by treaties to which African governments have agreed, would save many thousands or even millions of lives. But courts routinely rule against women on the basis of customary law.

Smooth Transition of Leadership

Zelophehad's legacy was assured, but what about that of Moses?

Not in terms of inheriting property, but the continuation of leadership after his death, which was coming soon.

Characteristically, Moses was concerned for his people rather than for himself. He asked the Lord to appoint a new leader, "who may go out before them and go in before them, who may lead them out and bring them in, that the congregation of the Lord may not be like sheep which have no shepherd" (Num. 27:17).

Having been a shepherd for many years (Ex. 2; 3), Moses knew how sheep need someone responsible to lead them, someone unlike me, who accidentally let a herd of sheep out of their pen and vainly tried to drive them back in. Moses had also shepherded Israel through the wilderness for decades. Without him, they could have perished several times.

As a wise individual in a powerful position, he could have simply selected an heir apparent of his choosing, someone close to him. But he did not trust his own wisdom for such a weighty decision. There was to be no nepotism and no politicking. Rather, the Lord Himself appointed the man whom He chose, just as He had chosen Moses.

The Lord's choice was Joshua, the assistant of Moses (Ex. 24; 32; 33; Num. 11), commander of the Israelite fighting men (Ex. 17) and one of the two faithful scouts (Num. 14). His work experience was impressive, but God named a more important qualification: "a man in whom is the Spirit" (Num. 27:18). It meant that he had already been allowing the Lord to guide and empower him through the Spirit as he had borne burdens and faced challenges. His track record with the Spirit showed that he would lead the Israelites where God intended, not off in another direction. Joshua would be a faithful shepherd, as Moses had been.

An elegantly simple, powerful ceremony commissioned Joshua as the new leader. Moses laid his hands on Joshua, thereby symbolically transferring authority to him so that he would immediately begin sharing power with Moses (Num. 27:18-23), an arrangement that would ensure a smooth transition after Moses died, without giving opportunity for someone to seize power, as Korah and company had tried to do.

If Moses were a king, Joshua would have been his coregent. But both received their orders from the divine King. Joshua would not talk face to face with the Lord as Moses had (cf. Num. 12:8; Deut. 34:10), but would receive directions through the divine oracle of Urim and Thummim administered by the high priest (Num. 27:21; cf. Ex. 28:30). Such a procedure would involve cooperation between civil and religious authority as a model for future leadership after Joshua.

Moses wanted to avoid a situation in which the Israelites would be like sheep without a shepherd. More than a millennium later Jesus did find His people in that condition: "But when He saw the multitudes, He was moved with compassion for them, because they were weary and scattered, like sheep having no shepherd" (Matt. 9:36). Jesus, the Good Shepherd, who has given His life for His "sheep," calls people to Himself and His "fold" (John 10) and rescues those who are lost (Luke 15:4-7). He also commissions leaders to take care of His "sheep" (John 21:16, 17). As we participate in His shepherding, may we have the faithful heart, guiding Spirit, protective toughness, and nurturing tenderness of Moses, Joshua, and Jesus!

Keeping Appointments With God

When I was a college student (theology and music majors) at Pacific Union College in Angwin, California, I was scheduled to speak at an evening worship service in the large chapel attached to one of the women's dormitories. Not having a regular appointment book, I wrote the information somewhere, but somehow lost track of it. A few months later I was practicing the piano at home and received a shocking phone call: The service had already started, but where was the speaker? I replied that they should sing a few extra songs and that I would be right there.

Quickly changing clothes, I jumped into my 1967 Saab. The car would not start. Panicked, I ran down a trail to the campus and up the hill to the chapel, arriving huffing, puffing, and sweaty just in time to see hundreds of students walking away. Among them was the sister of a girl I was dating. Thoroughly chagrined, I avoided her and everyone else, walked home, and immediately put the Saab up for sale.

When you make appointments, especially with the Lord, you need to be organized. It helps to have an appointment calendar. That is what Numbers 28 and 29 are. Leviticus 23 already gave instructions for observance of weekly Sabbaths and special yearly festival events. Numbers 28 and 29 provide a comprehensive list of sacrifices that the Israelite community must offer to the Lord every day, every Sabbath, on the first of every month, and at the yearly festivals.

Regular sacrificial worship at fixed sacred times would remind the Israelites of their covenant relationship with the Lord. Placement of this list here in the book of Numbers reinforces the idea that the younger generation about to possess the Promised Land should keep their just and merciful Lord uppermost in their minds and hearts.

Foundational to the entire sacrificial system was the burnt offering of a male lamb every morning and another as the last sacrifice of the day in the evening (Num. 28:1-8; echoing Ex. 29:38-42). Grain and drink offerings accompanied each one to make it a full meal for the Lord (cf. Num. 15). Whatever else happened was in addition to the regular burnt offering. It served as the daily "food" of the Lord (Num. 28:2), just as other ancient Near Eastern peoples gave their deities two meals per day, the same number of meals that humans ate in those days. Non-Israelites, however, thought that their deities actually needed human food:

"In the Ugaritic myth of the god Baal, when the god 'Ilu (El) sees the goddess 'Aṭiratu coming to him, he says to her: 'Are you really hungry (because) you've been wandering?' In the Babylonian epic Atrahasis, the gods suffer from hunger and thirst during the great Flood because there are no humans to offer them sacrifices. So when Atrahasis (the 'Noah' figure) subsequently offers his sacrifice, the gods smell the offering (compare Gen. 8:20, 21) and crowd around like flies. Unlike Yahweh, they enjoy the smell because it promises an end to their hunger. In a prayer, the Hittite king Muršili II pointedly used the gods' need for food as an argument to plead that they remove a plague from his land lest they suffer due to lack of humans to serve them. By contrast, the God of Israel does not need human sacrifices to nourish him (Ps. 50:12, 13)."*

Unlike the pagan offerings, those the Israelites presented were only tokens of faith in Him and fellowship with Him. He is the source and sustainer of all physical, mental, and spiritual life. So the souls of the sons of Korah thirst for him (Ps. 42:2) and their heart and flesh sing for joy (Ps. 84:2).

The foundational sacrifice was a lamb. So it is not surprising that Isaiah's towering "suffering servant poem" compares God's suffering Messiah to a lamb who endures in silence for all of us who have gone astray like sheep (Isa. 53:6, 7). It is also fitting that John the Baptist first publicly announced Jesus as "the Lamb of God who takes away the sin of the world!" (John 1:29). It was as though he said: Here is the One who fulfills the entire Israelite sacrificial system!

Basic Sabbath rest on the seventh day of every week was not a ceremonial observance dependent on the ritual system. It preceded the ritual system and celebrated the Creation "birthday" of Planet Earth (Gen. 2:2, 3; Ex. 16:22-30; 20:11; 31:17). However, the ritual system honored the Sabbath by the sacrifice of two additional lambs (Num. 28:9, 10) and by renewal of the "bread of the presence" ("shewbread") inside the sanctuary (Lev. 24:8).

At new moons, which began the months, the priests presented a group of additional burnt offerings and one purification ("sin") offering. Along with their grain and drink accompaniments, they presumably supplemented the regular morning burnt offering (Num. 28:11-15). New moons were significant because the Israelite calendar was basically a lunar one, built on the monthly orbit of the moon around the earth (Ex. 12:2), but periodically adjusted to fit the yearly cycle of the earth around the sun.

On the fourth day of Creation the Lord had assigned to the heavenly bodies the function of structuring human time on Planet Earth by serving "for signs and seasons, and for days and years" (Gen. 1:14). So worship at new moons would have celebrated the Lord as the Creator and maintainer of our solar system and of human time. While Sabbaths also honor the Creator and structure time (weeks), they had their origin in the Lord's example and word (Gen. 2:2, 3; Ex. 20:8-11), rather than marking the movement of any heavenly body.

It was important for the Israelites periodically to reaffirm God's creative lordship over the heavenly bodies, because other ancient Near Eastern peoples worshipped the sun, moon, planets, and stars as deities. In fact, Abraham's family came from a moon-worshipping background in Mesopotamia.

Isaiah 66:22, 23 prophesies that all people will worship God on new moons and Sabbaths in "the new heavens and the new earth." Since the basic meaning of new moons and weekly Sabbaths is to celebrate God as the Creator, their relevance will outlive the problem of sin. In his vision of the new earth John saw another monthly natural event that is the gift of the Creator: "the tree of life, which bore twelve fruits, each tree yielding its fruit every month. The leaves of the tree were for the healing of the nations" (Rev. 22:2).

Numbers 28:16 to the end of chapter 29 lists additional sacrifices to be performed on the yearly festival occasions (cf. Lev. 23:4-43). Spring festivals included Passover and Unleavened Bread, and the Festival of Weeks (Pentecost). Autumn festivals consisted of the Festival of Trumpets, the Day of Atonement, and the Festival of Booths ("Tabernacles"). Each occasion had additional burnt offerings and their accompaniments, plus one purification offering to make atonement for the people. Burnt offerings also provided atonement (Lev. 1:4; 16:24), but purification offerings focused especially on removal of sin (for example, Lev. 4).

Burnt offerings on behalf of the entire Israelite community every day of the year, plus additional burnt and purification offerings on festival occasions (including the Day of Atonement), provided God's people with a kind of blanket atonement coverage. It is true that individuals also had to bring their own sacrifices to the sanctuary and receive forgiveness from God (Lev. 4; 5). But the public sacrifices covered them before they could get to the sanctuary. Remember that when the Israelites spread out in the land of Canaan, God required their males to come to the sanctuary only three times a year: for the festivals of Unleavened Bread, Weeks/Harvest, and Booths/Ingathering (Ex. 23:14-17; 34:22-24).

The relationship between corporate/community and individual atonement taught by the Israelite sacrificial system helps us to understand the connection between the blanket availability of atonement that Christ freely provided for everyone when He died on the cross (Rom. 5:15, 16; 2 Cor. 5:19) and our individual experience of atonement when we receive Christ's gift by faith (Rom. 5:17; 2 Cor. 5:20; Eph. 2:8). When Christ died, He bought back our world (John 12:31) so that its inhabitants could survive, and gave everyone the opportunity to have eternal life, on condition that they would personally believe in Him (John 3:16). If Christ had not died like that, there would have been no basis for the continued existence of the human race. Generally people who reject Christ and scoff at Him do not realize that without His sacrifice they would not even be alive.

When we sin, we are under obligation to confess so that we can receive forgiveness and cleansing (Lev. 5:1, 5, 6; 1 John 1:9). But what Christ did on the cross for everyone covers us before we have the opportunity to acknowledge our guilt.

This answers a question that has perplexed many people: What happens if I die immediately after sinning, without the opportunity to confess? Suppose that you are driving and someone cuts you off in a rude and dangerous manner. Overcome by unrighteous indignation, you make a gesture or say something that you shouldn't. Then BAM! Your life ends in a tragic accident. Are you eternally lost because the last thing you did was sin, and you did not confess because you died at that moment? No, if you have continued to accept Christ as your Savior, His sacrifice would cover you until you could confess. If you are unable to confess, you would not be lost on that basis. God so loved the world that He gave His only Son (John 3:16). He isn't waiting until we make a mistake so that He can drop the axe at that instant, rub His hands in glee, and exult: "Got 'em!"

The festivals celebrated agricultural and historical aspects of the relationship between God and His people. Through His creative power He provided them with food at the early harvest (Weeks) and later harvest (Booths). The lavish outlay of sacrifices at the Festival of Booths gave Him special thanks at the end of the harvest season. And through the Lord's redemptive power (which includes His control over creation) He set them free from Egypt (Passover and Unleavened Bread) and sustained them in the wilderness (Booths). He was acclaimed as their divine king (Trumpets), and He judged between His loyal and disloyal subjects when the justice of His treatment of faulty people was vindicated (Day of Atonement).

Israelites showed their loyalty to the Lord on the Day of Atonement by humbling themselves through self-denial (fasting, etc.) and focusing on the final phase of atonement for them by abstaining

144

from all work (Num. 29:7; cf. Lev. 16:29-31; 23:26-32). The ceremonial sabbath of the Day of Atonement was like the weekly Sabbath in that Israelites were not to do any work. Other ceremonial sabbaths allowed for doing some work (such as housework) that was not part of a person's occupation (Num. 28:18, 25, 26; 29:1, 12, 35).

While we cannot keep the biblical festivals today because the ritual system to which they belonged no longer exists, we can learn a lot from them. It would be good for us to set apart special times to celebrate God's sovereignty and the sustaining care and deliverance that He provides. Jesus has already provided us with a transformed Passover—the Lord's Supper—to help us remember the redemption that He has provided through His once-for-all sacrifice. By partaking of the grain and drink accompaniments to sacrifice, which represent Him, we accept His sacrifice as our Passover Lamb (Matt. 26:17-19, 26-29; 1 Cor. 11:23-26; 5:7; cf. Ex. 12).

When Promises Cannot Be Kept

The daughter of missionary parents had moved back to the United States from India.

Now she had a serious boyfriend and was sure they would get married several years in the future, when they had finished their education. In her excitement the girl promised an Indian friend that she would be maid of honor at the wedding. The romance progressed much faster than expected, and the couple married less than a year later. At this point in their lives they had no money at all to fly the friend from India to participate in the wedding. So the bride wrote a letter of deep apology and had to ask another friend to be maid of honor. The Indian girl did not write back and never communicated with her again.

What happens if you make a promise but then discover that you are not able to keep it?

Such a scenario is a recipe for frustration and hurt feelings. If your promise is to the Lord, the situation is even more serious. Numbers 30 helps people get out of this kind of dilemma.

To a modern reader the divine instructions in Numbers 30 could appear sexist. If a man or an independent woman (widowed or divorced) makes a vow to the Lord or takes an oath, that person must absolutely keep his or her promise. However, the vow or oath of a young woman dwelling in her father's house or of a wife living with her husband is subject to the approval of the father or husband on the day that he first hears it. If he says nothing at that point, she is bound by her obligation. But if he objects and does not permit her to carry out the vow or oath, it releases her from her promise, and the Lord promises automatically to forgive her. It is the only instance of forgiveness by statute in Israelite law.

Is the Bible prejudiced against women here? The fact that independent women are treated like men indicates that the issue is not simply gender. Rather, it is the social relationship between a woman and her father or husband, who has jurisdiction over her in the area of vows and oaths that could affect him.

Israelite society regarded men as responsible for legal matters, including transactions involving property. So if a daughter or wife took a vow or oath regarding transfer of property, including to the Lord, she would likely need her man's cooperation in order to fulfill her promise. If she put pressure on him to cooperate and he did so grudgingly, there could be resentment in the home. Should he refuse to cooperate, she would not be able to fulfill her vow, and would be guilty of a serious crime. God prevented these problems by releasing women from obligations if their men registered unwillingness to go along with them.

"Any vow or any binding oath to deny herself, her husband may allow to stand, or her husband may nullify" (Num. 30:13, NRSV). The passage refers to physical self-denial, which could include a vow to abstain from sexual relations for a period of time. Obviously, keeping such a promise would require the husband's willingness, and he could be resentful if he felt forced into a situation that he did not want. Again, God made a way to avoid unhappiness between men and women. Similarly, the apostle Paul recognized the need for husbands and wives to cooperate in the area of sexuality:

"The husband should give to his wife her conjugal rights, and likewise the wife to her husband. For the wife does not have authority over her own body, but the husband does; likewise the husband does not have authority over his own body, but the wife does. Do not deprive one another except perhaps by agreement for a set time, to devote yourselves to prayer, and then come together again, so that Satan may not tempt you because of your lack of self-control" (1 Cor. 7:3-5, NRSV).

Two aspects of Numbers 30 are remarkable. First, the Lord could have insisted on His own rights as deity and king by requiring fulfillment of all vows to Him and oaths taken in His name, regardless of consequences to anyone else in the family. But He was more concerned for harmony in Israelite homes than for His own rights.

Second, the Lord worked with an ancient society. He did not make the society, but regulated it in order to improve conditions and solve problems. Although He is supremely powerful, He did not engage in social engineering by trying to overthrow the patriarchal way of doing things. In modern times we have seen how destructive social engineering can be. Forcing Russian and Chinese societies into the mold of Communism destroyed the lives of many millions of people. Estimates of Chinese deaths under the leadership of Chairman Mao range as high as 75 million. My wife and I recently spent several weeks in Romania while teaching extension courses, and we saw how this beautiful country and its society have not yet fully recovered from the ravages of Communism that ended with a revolution in 1989.

As we seek to reach people of various cultures with the message of God's love, we can learn from His wise and gentle approach. In the process of receiving Him and living according to His principles, others do not need to become exactly like us. Genuine loyalty to the Lord can flourish in a wide variety of cultural contexts.

---

* Roy Gane, "Leviticus," in *Zondervan Illustrated Bible Backgrounds Commentary on the Old Testament* (Grand Rapids: Zondervan, forthcoming), vol. 1, on Lev. 1:9. Note that "Yahweh"-Jehovah, the personal name of Israel's God, usually translated "the Lord."

LOOKING IN THE REARVIEW MIRROR, WHILE MOVING AHEAD

(Numbers 31–36)

Divine Vengeance

Before Moses died, the Lord wanted him to take care of some unfinished business: "Take vengeance on the Midianites for the children of Israel" (Num. 31:2). God's command raises two questions. First, why should retributive justice fall on the Midianites and not the Moabites as well? Second, why did Moses need to be in charge of this operation?

Regarding the first question, Moabite women had participated in seducing Israelites into immorality and idolatrous worship of the Baal of Peor (Num. 25:1-3). But it was the additional role of the Midianites, represented by the daughter of a Midianite chieftain, that brought the apostasy to a climax and apparently precipitated the plague that killed 24,000 Israelites (verses 6-9, 14-18). The Israelites who died were part of a guilty community, but by tempting God's people, the Midianites shared their guilt and responsibility for their deaths. The Lord had told the Israelites not to harass the Moabites, who would retain their land as neighbors of Israel (Deut. 2:9), but He had not protected the Midianites in the same way.

By holding the Midianites accountable and ordering retributive justice upon them, the Lord showed what He thinks of those who destroy people by tempting and deceiving them into sin. The grand-daddy of all tempters is Satan himself (Rev. 12:9; cf. Gen. 3; Matt. 4), who will ultimately perish in a lake of fire (Rev. 20). Nobody else who "causes an abomination or a lie" or "loves and practices a lie" will ultimately be saved (Rev. 21:27; 22:15). This excludes from salvation those who profit from the deception of pleasurable poisons, including producers and merchants of illegal drugs and legal alcoholic beverages and tobacco. Also it eliminates those who seduce people into immorality, such as prostitutes, pimps, producers of pornography, and many involved in the film industry. Another destructive deception is the occult (practices relating to dark supernatural forces), which is reaching its dark and devilish fingers into many homes through its advocates in various media and religious systems.

God's grace can and does redeem human tempters (who themselves are deceived) if they are willing to accept His gift of life and cleansing through Christ's sacrifice. But if they persist in ruining other people, their destruction is sure. The warning is also for us. Even if we do not tempt for a career, perhaps we mislead others once in a while. We would do well to ask ourselves whether people are better or worse off as a result of our influence.

Now we turn to the question of why Moses should direct the dirty work of punishing the Midianites and eliminating their threat to Israel. One reason would be that the Midianites had committed their crime against the Israelites when Moses was leading them. Thus it made sense for Israel under him to punish them, so that everyone would clearly see the connection between the two events.

There may be an additional factor. The Midianites were descended from Abraham through Keturah, the wife he took after Sarah died (Gen. 25:1, 2, 4). So they were relatives of the Israelites, along with the Moabites, Ammonites, and Edomites. But Moses was much more closely related to at least one branch of the widely spread Midianite people through his wife, Zipporah, the daughter of a priest of Midian (Ex. 2), who was a worshipper of the true God. By punishing idolatrous Midianites himself, Moses would demonstrate that when the Lord mandates removal of evil that threatens His people, loyal followers of God do not even spare relatives (cf. Ex. 32:25-29). Rather, they bear the first responsibility to put a stop to the danger. Moses later articulated this principle with regard to those who try to entice God's people into idolatry:

"If your brother, the son of your mother, your son or your daughter, the wife of your bosom, or your friend who is as your own soul, secretly entices you, saying, 'Let us go and serve other gods,'. . . you shall not consent to him or listen to him, nor shall your eye pity him, nor shall you spare him or conceal him; but you shall surely kill him; your hand shall be first against him to put him to death, and afterward the hand of all the people" (Deut. 13:6-9).

The campaign against the Midianites was holy war to carry out divine retributive justice on the international level, not aggression in cold blood for the sake of conquest. It would be a warning to other nations tempted to wipe out His chosen people, His channel of revelation in the world. To show that it was holy war, Phinehas the priest accompanied the troops with some sacred utensils and the priestly signal trumpets (Num. 31:6). The presence of Phinehas, who had put an end to the plague at the time of the Baal Peor apostasy by executing Zimri and Cozbi (Num. 25), specifically linked that event to the war on Midian.

The Israelites attacked the guilty Midianites and killed all their males, including the five kings of the Midianite tribal confederation, as well as Balaam (Num. 31:7, 8); but other Midianites must have survived (see Judges 6-8). Because of the Lord's protection, not one Israelite soldier died in the war, as the military officers acknowledged with a special thank offering to Him (Num. 31:48-54).

The Israelite troops spared the Midianite women and children, but Moses ordered that only the young virgin girls be kept alive. The women were dangerous and guilty because they had lured the Israelites into lethal apostasy at the advice of Balaam (Num. 31:9-18). Young boys could be dangerous because they would carry on Midianite identity and could seek revenge (compare Haman, apparently a descendant of Agag the Amalekite [1 Sam. 15; Esther 3-7]). On the other hand, Israel could safely assimilate virgin girls into the nation through marriage (cf. Deut. 25:10-14).

The whole episode sounds frightfully brutal to us. Earlier at Arad and later at Jericho and other places, devotion to utter destruction did not even spare virgin girls (Num. 21:1-3; Joshua 6, etc.; Israel also destroyed animals along with other property). Without question the Bible clearly indicates that the Lord commanded such extermination. Some modern interpreters want to deny this, saying that Moses and the Israelites were mistaken when they thought that it was God's will for them to annihilate whole people groups. But if Moses and other prophets misrepresented the Lord in this area, how can we believe in other biblical reports and teachings, such as Creation, the faith of Abraham, the Exodus story, and so on? Paul said that all of Scripture is inspired and profitable (2 Tim. 3:16). It is all or nothing. If we start picking and choosing what we like, as we do at a cafeteria, we create even more problems and eventually end up with nothing to believe.

The Lord has the right to put an end to corrupt groups of people (Sodom and Gomorrah [Gen. 19]) and even entire civilizations (the pre-Flood and end-time worlds [Gen. 7; Rev. 19; 20]) by whatever means He chooses, whether by water, fire, or Israelites. His corporate executions have included women and children. Perhaps even these children were morally tainted beyond redemption, or maybe there was another reason. God knows enough to make the right decision for the big picture and the long run. We do not. Therefore, we are not qualified to judge God's justice (cf. Job 38-42) and should humbly leave the secret things with Him (Deut. 29:29) until we have access to His heavenly records (1 Cor. 6:2, 3; Rev. 20:4). Faith is accepting that He knows best and that we can safely entrust ourselves to Him. Job affirmed: "Though He slay me, yet will I trust Him" (Job 13:15).

Conflict Management

The remaining chapters of the book of Numbers involve plans for Israelite settlement: the allocation of Transjordanian territories (Num. 32), the need to clear out all Canaanites thoroughly (Num. 33), the distribution of Canaan territory among Israelite tribes (Num. 34), the establishment of the Levite cities, including cities of refuge (Num. 35), and the requirement for daughters inheriting property to marry within their clans in order to keep land holdings intact (Num. 36).

The Israelites destroyed the settlements of the Midianites (Num.

151

31:10), but did not occupy the area where they dwelt. The nation of Israel was about to cross the Jordan to possess Canaan, which was west of the river. However, they had already taken possession of the territories of Sihon, king of the Amorites, and Og, king of Bashan (Num. 21). Since these areas were east of the Jordan, they were not part of the Promised Land. Once the Israelites had occupied Canaan, they planned to abandon the lands of Sihon and Og. But the tribes of Reuben and Gad were ranchers and saw that the areas were perfect for raising cattle. So they asked Moses and the other leaders if they could make their home on the range there, rather than settling in Canaan (Num. 32:1-5).

It was true that if some tribes settled east of the Jordan, it would provide more space for other tribes on the west. But Moses delivered a sizzling rebuke because he initially took the request as a cowardly and rebellious way to get out of helping the other Israelites conquer Canaan. Such a move would discourage the rest of the people, just as the 10 scouts had done to everyone at Kadesh, and another generation would perish (verses 6-15). The Reubenites and Gadites saw the point and proposed that they get their families and livestock settled east of the Jordan, and then their men would cross over the Jordan and lead the other Israelites into battle in order to help them conquer the Promised Land (verses 16-19).

Moses agreed to the proposed conditions and gave the eastern lands to Reuben, Gad, and half the tribe of Manasseh (verses 20-42). However, he sternly warned them: "But if you do not do so, you will have sinned against the Lord; and know that your sin will overtake you" (verse 23, Tanakh). He meant: "Know that the Lord will hold you accountable and will see to it that your sin of breaking your promise results in fitting punishment." His warning may sound severe, but once some tribes had already received their inheritance, their only incentive to risk their lives in order to help the other Israelites would be loyalty to the Lord and to the nation. It would be like paying a worker before he does the job.

Numbers 32 is a lesson in managing conflict through the principles of forthright communication, respect for the perspectives of others, and flexibility. Some people had a bright idea. But others read the motivation as selfish and saw a harmful result. Rather than rebelling, trying to get their way through another means, or sulking and criticizing, the group with the idea continued communication by bringing an expanded and modified proposal that met the legitimate concerns of the other party and showed that the motivation was not selfish after all. Their proposal, which did not compromise the well-being of anyone, was accepted and implemented as a win-win outcome.

We need the perspectives of others, especially when they see things that we don't. We also need unity and high morale. When (not if) we have differences, whether in our homes, churches, schools, or other institutions, the way we work through them has a huge impact on our success or even our survival.

It is true that in some situations in which we listen to people and take their reasons into account, we still must make choices that do not please them. However, we should not let our egos or desires for personal gain get in the way of settling conflicts when peaceful resolution is possible. Do you stand to gain something big? Its greatness probably does not compare with homes for entire Israelite tribes. Are you an important person with tremendous authority? You are definitely not as important or powerful as Moses. So don't just throw your weight around because you can. Being reasonable and flexible will not compromise your leadership.

As God Has Led Us in the Past

While planning for the future, it is wise to remember past experience, just as you glance in the rearview mirror while you drive ahead. As we move on in life, it is easy to lose sight of the big picture. We have deadlines to meet, appointments to keep, bills and debts to pay, home repairs to carry out, and so on. The stress can be depressing. But let us pause to remember what it was like when we were penniless students, living hand to mouth on low wages for long hours of exhausting work, renting a small apartment, and all the while trying to cope with the relentless pressure of hard study. Then we realize that we have come a long way!

In the midst of plans for possessing Canaan, Numbers 33:1-49 summarizes the incredible journey of the Israelites from Egypt to the border of the Promised Land. The long list of places, which Moses recorded in his diary, serves as a reminder of God's leading. It is much longer than the Lord wished it to be, but His people needed a lot of extra time for remedial work before their faith training was adequate. He did not grade on the curve or advance His students to the next grade just because they reached a certain age. Their faith had to come up to a necessary standard through receiving His gifts and learning to cooperate with Him. Without strong enough faith, they would fail to trust Him at a time of danger, and all could be lost. Leading soldiers into battle before they are ready is a recipe for disaster.

Even if the Israelites won battles, they could still lose the war and throw away all that their arduous journey had gained if they would not follow the Lord's directions to finish the job of totally driving out all the Canaanites and destroying their places of worship (Num. 33:50-54). "But if you do not drive out the inhabitants of the land from before you, then it shall be that those whom you let remain shall be irritants in your eyes and thorns in your sides, and they shall harass you in the land where you dwell. Moreover it shall be that I will do to you as I thought to do to them" (verses 55, 56).

Anyone who questions God's wisdom needs only to read the book of Judges, which recounts what happened after the Israelites under Joshua initially conquered most of the land.

The Israelite tribes lost their momentum and, relying on their own wisdom, found it easier to live with remaining pockets of Canaanites than to finish them off. As a result, God's people fell into apostasy and were oppressed, just as the Lord had said. It postponed solid peace for hundreds of years.

In order to serve as God's channel of revelation to the world, His people are in the world, but they are not to be of the world (John 15:19; 17:14-16). They must be distinct, or the world will not see the difference. The Israelites had trouble maintaining their boundaries. It was hard enough to be surrounded by idolatrous nations, but when they tolerated and even made friends with idolators in their midst, the temptation to assimilate and be like everyone else was simply too great for them.

154

Today many accuse God of being too harsh. However, they do not take into account the situation that He was dealing with, including the childish level of His people's faith. Perhaps an analogy will help a bit. Do you want your children addicted to narcotics? No. Such drugs would destroy their lives. So do you desire for your children to make friends with drug dealers, who would try to get your children hooked on drugs? Of course not! Would you permit a drug dealer to live in your house along with you and your children? Don't be ridiculous!

What if the drug dealer lived in the house before you moved in, and he refused to leave? Would you take the trouble to evict him? Well . . . he is dangerous and would seek revenge. Then would you turn him in to the police so that they could jail him and prevent him from harming anyone? Of course! What if you knew that he had murdered people and would be executed? Would you still turn him in? Who should be protected—the human predator or your children? It is not possible to defend both. The criminal previously had the right to live in the house, but no longer.

Hopefully what God did is making better sense by now. Now, to what higher human authorities could He hand over the criminals living with His Israelite children? There were none, and there were no jails, either. The highest authority was God, so He had to judge and order the execution Himself. His children needed a safe place to live, and the Canaanites had forfeited their right to continue living in the land. If the Israelites got hooked on the addictions of the Canaanites, they would also lose the land (cf. Lev. 18:24-30; 20:22-26).

Refuge Until the High Priest's Death Brings Freedom

Two and a half tribes already had their inheritance to the east of the Jordan River (Num. 32). Nine and a half tribes would receive territories in Canaan when the Israelites conquered it.

Division of this land among them would be equitably determined by lot and administered by national and tribal leaders (Num. 34; cf. Joshua 13-19). Rather than receiving one territory, however, the tribe of Levi would be assigned cities, surrounded by some pastureland, within the areas of the other tribes (Num. 35:1-8). The

Levites received their livelihood from their service to the sanctuary (Num. 18:20-24), so they did not need extensive farmlands. Distributing the religious leaders among the other tribes would tend to unify the nation under God.

God designated six of the Levitical towns in various parts of the nation as cities of refuge to which accidental manslayers could flee. There were three cities on each side of the Jordan River (Num. 35:6, 9-15).

Accidents happen. One day when I was working for a building contractor to put my bride and me through school, I was helping to demolish a temporary wooden loading dock. Swinging hard with a big 28-ounce hammer, I lost my grip, and the hammer flew through the air toward a man's head. He saw it and swiftly ducked just in time, or he could easily have died. I never saw him move so rapidly before or after this incident. Whew! That was way too close!

If Israelites accidentally killed somebody, they could flee to the nearest city of refuge and receive a fair trial. But if they did not flee, a relative of the deceased would avenge the death, whether it was intentional or accidental, by killing the individual. Those who reached a city of refuge and were judged to be innocent of intentional murder would be safe from the avenger if they remained at the city of refuge until the death of the high priest. After that they could return home (verses 22-28).

Those who committed first-degree murder, as shown by circumstances (use of a weapon, ambush, prior enmity, etc.), had no asylum or ransom. The law required capital punishment in such a case (verses 16-21, 31). "So you shall not pollute the land where you are; for blood defiles the land, and no atonement can be made for the land, for the blood that is shed on it, except by the blood of him who shed it" (verse 33).

Several aspects of this passage sound strange to us. First, why were cities of refuge even necessary? Why didn't the law simply forbid blood vengeance by relatives? Here again, we see that the Lord solved problems within the framework of an existing culture rather than carrying out social engineering (cf. Num. 30 regarding vows of women). The role of the avenger of blood, a relative with a strong vested interest in seeing to it that justice was done, was an ingrained tradition deeply rooted in the culture and worldview of the people. It would be difficult to stamp out this custom so that accidental manslayers would really be safe. There was nothing wrong with an avenger executing a first-degree murderer (Num. 35:21). The problem was how to save accidental killers. It was not safe to rely upon an avenger, driven by the passion of grief, to distinguish between intentional and accidental death. It would be conflict of interest for such a prosecutor also to fulfill the role of defense attorney.

Second, in what sense did murder defile the land? This was moral defilement, like idolatry or sexual immorality (cf. Lev. 18; 20 regarding Molech worship, adultery, incest, homosexual activity, and bestiality), not physical ritual impurity, which could be remedied through ritual (such as corpse contamination [Num. 19]). The land was "defiled" in the sense that if a group of people committed too many serious moral crimes while living there, it would "vomit" them out—that is, the Lord would see to it that they were expelled (Lev. 18:24-30; 20:22-26). Ultimately that is what happened, so that Israel and Judah went into exile (2 Kings 17, 25; 2 Chron. 36; the books of Jeremiah and Ezekiel).

Third, why was an accidental manslayer restricted to a city of refuge, and why did the death of the high priest release him (Num. 35:25-28)? Although the damage caused by a manslayer was accidental, he had taken the life of a person made in the image of God. Human life is sacred, which explains why assault causing a permanent physical defect was such a serious offense in biblical law, punishable by the law of retaliation (Lev. 24:19, 20). The same word for "permanent defect" in the law of assault elsewhere refers to defects that diminished sacred life and thereby disqualified male descendants of Aaron from holy office as priests (Lev. 21:16-23). An inadvertent or accidental sin was a sin nonetheless, but the Lord provided atonement for it (cf. Lev. 4). Even in the case of accidental killing, life is so valuable that only a human death can atone for it. But in place of the manslayer's death (cf. Num. 35:33), the Lord accepted the natural death of the high priest.

The death of a high priest as a kind of atonement that provides freedom shows up in the New Testament, but this time it is not a natural death: "But Christ came as High Priest of the good things to come, with the greater and more perfect tabernacle not made with hands, that is, not of this creation. Not with the blood of goats and calves, but with His own blood He entered the Most Holy Place once for all, having obtained eternal redemption" (Heb. 9:11, 12).

Conclusion

The book of Numbers ends with the marriages of the daughters of Zelophehad (Num. 36). After the intense drama of conflicts in the wilderness, victory over nations, and allocation of territories among tribes, it seems like an anticlimax. But it is fitting to focus here on the connection between the past—Zelophehad and his generation, and the new generation of his daughters, who were about to enter their inheritance. Out of the ashes of mistakes left behind in the wilderness comes a glorious future for families of the divine Redeemer!

We are on the borders of our Promised Land. We too have years of mistakes to leave behind. And we too have the privilege of stepping across the threshold into a better home. Will we take our families with us? Will we wholeheartedly follow the Lord, as Caleb and Joshua did? Do we want heavenly mansions enough to leave our tents behind? Do we desire to talk with our Shekinah Lord face to face more than anything else in the world?

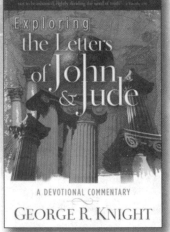
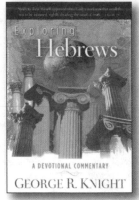
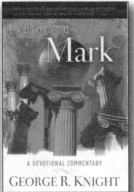
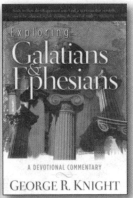
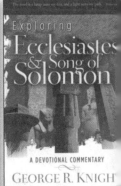